Communication for the Severely and Profoundly Handicapped

Maurice Dayan and Beryl Harper,
Pinecrest State School, Louisiana
Julia S. Molloy, University of San Diego
Byrn T. Witt, Rolling Meadows, Illinois

W9-CNA-015

LOVE PUBLISHING COMPANY
Denver, Colorado 80222

Copyright © 1977 Love Publishing Company
Printed in the U.S.A.
ISBN 0-89108-064-3
Library of Congress Catalog Card Number 76-62662
10 9 8 7 6 5 4 3 2 1

Dedication

Being with a child who does not understand what you say and who cannot make you understand what he wants is a heartbreaking situation. When you take care of such a child, you know just how hard life must be for him. You are "mama" to him, and he looks to you to take care of him. You know him better than anyone else because you see his faith in you every day and you are with him more than anyone else. You own his trust in grownups.

Many of us have attempted to learn some answers about retarded development but only you, the daily "mama," can apply these answers directly to each child. You are quick to see a tiny clue, and only you are able to rejoice in a tiny gain as it takes place. When you first experience the smile of success that comes over a child's face when he knows he has done something that you have been trying to teach him to do, you will feel rewarded and privileged to be the one who has made the gain possible.

To work with children who are profoundly retarded takes the patience of Job, the strength of David, and the wisdom of Solomon. These virtues are built into those who choose to work with such youngsters.

This book is dedicated to helping you to learn how important it is to have patience, to encourage you to seek the strength you need to keep trying when things seem to be at a standstill, and to share with you what knowledge has come from the experiences of others.

You are entrusted with the privilege of helping a child to achieve a more comfortable life. You are mama to each child in the finest sense and in the blind faith of a child's understanding of that word.

You are by his side, helping him, making him feel worthwhile, When you and the child both feel worthwhile, the job provides you with an ease and comfort you can get only when you are sharing your love and strength with someone who needs you very much. As his special person, you can do for such a child that which no one else can do. Do your job proudly — you have no rival for the faith of a child you really want to help.

Contents

Foreword

The education and training of the severely and profoundly handicapped individual have at last become a challenge to those who work with him, rather than an exercise in futility. This change in attitude has come about largely through a revised conception of retardation; one founded on advances in behavioral science.

We now think of a severely or profoundly handicapped individual as one who is developmentally retarded as a result of an interactional history that is far below that of a normal individual. The factors limiting a person's history are usually a combination of deviations and subnormalities in the person's social and physical environment and in his or her own biological makeup. With this view of retardation, it is natural to ask, "What can we as teachers do to enhance the learning history of an individual and thereby help him to develop further and to lead a more interesting life?"

This book offers one practical answer: We can use our knowledge of applied behavior analysis to help these handicapped individuals to communicate more effectively. In so doing, we give the individual the means to participate in exciting social activities and help him to share the many wonders of our culture.

This volume should help provide the severely and profoundly handicapped individual with the means to enter a new world. How much each individual will develop is an open question, for we have no meaningful way of measuring a person's psychological potential. We can find out only by providing the individual with new programs and teaching procedures such as those described in this book.

Sidney W. Bijou
University of Arizona
Tucson, Arizona

Introduction

This manual is the result of the work of many direct care employees working together with professionals who were convinced that a communication program could be developed for profoundly and severely retarded persons. It is the outgrowth of several years of experience at Pinecrest State School, where success has been realized in the training of profoundly retarded residents in self-help skills through the use of special training techniques and behavior shaping.

A definitive description of these techniques is available in Bensberg (1965) and the companion film *Teaching the Mentally Retarded — A Positive Approach.* The literature concerning the practical application of behavior shaping techniques has grown from a few early articles (Ellis, 1963; Dayan, 1964; and Watson, 1967) to an annotated bibliography (Gardner & Watson, 1969) that contains over 200 articles.

Encouraged by the success of reward training in developing self-help skills, Cecil Colwell, Director of Community Living, and Dr. Maurice Dayan, Director of Training and Research, began to contemplate the feasibility of using these techniques for language development.

As Project Directors of a Hospital Improvement Grant, they broadened their goals of training to include language development and formed a team of consultants to assist them.

The consultant team was composed of Julia Molloy, Byrn Witt, and Alice Sims. Their goal was to develop a language development training guide and suitable procedures that could be taught to cottage parents and cottage trainers. The staff of Pinecrest, who were familiar with reward training techniques, would redesign the language training procedures into a communication shaping program. A select number of cottage parents would be trained in using the program. The consultants would organize language evaluation procedures while the cottage parents tried the procedures with groups of profoundly retarded residents.

In the beginning, Pinecrest did not have a speech therapy department; therefore, Effie Bryant, area supervisor, and Linda George, cottage parent, became key personnel in the project. They had the actual responsibility of implementing the proposed techniques. Alice Sims, Louisiana State Audiologist Consultant, was involved in early pilot work. Pat Aycock, supervisor of the Employee's Reward Training Center, provided invaluable information related to the use of lip and jaw exercises.

A year after the program began, Beryl Harper, a speech pathologist, was recruited. In two short years, besides developing an excellent speech and hearing department, Mrs. Harper also became an important contributor to this specific project.

This book resulted from the program at Pinecrest State school. It is designed for direct care aides who work with severely and profoundly handicapped individuals. It is designed to increase skills in communication and language shaping and to help the aide learn what activities need to be emphasized and when to proceed to a more difficult activity. Finally, this manual was conceived and developed with the concept that the potential of the profoundly retarded has yet to be determined, and that every retarded individual has a right to experiences and training that might lead to a higher level of independent living.

The techniques emphasized throughout the manual are based upon the ABC (Acceptable Behavior Change) technique, described by Barrett (1973). The ABC technique utilizes the concept of step-by-step training, beginning with present ability and training to the next behavior level or acceptable approximation by the use of rewards.

After an initial visit to the institution by the consultant team, the project began. A group of eight boys was selected because of their management difficulties. They were evaluated by the language consultants to determine the individual level of language development, the hearing of each child was studied, and difficulties with speech mechanisms were identified.

Individually-prescribed language programs were written for each boy, together with a rough draft of the material on communication, gaining a child's attention, and total body activity. The consultants demonstrated the activities to the cottage parents. The hospital improvement project staff incorporated reward training techniques into the language activities. Daily and weekly progress notes were kept. As a result of these early experiences, some of the language activities were modified or dropped, and new activities were added, always utilizing reward training techniques. Subsequently, a rough draft of the material on tongue, lip, and jaw exercises was added. It was more than six months from the beginning of the program that receptive language activities were implemented. Finally, after approximately one year, some of the boys were ready for expressive language activities.

All material underwent changes as a result of the trial-and-error use of the language activities suggested by the consultants. Through their initiative, ingenuity, and at times, sheer genius, the cottage parents and hospital improvement program staff have always found a way to achieve the goals of the suggested language activities with the use of reward training techniques.

As the training techniques were refined and progress was noted with the initial eight boys, the techniques were utilized with residents of other cottages. A recording system was developed to measure the progress of each resident. Throughout the development of the materials it was the cottage parents who determined whether an activity should remain, be changed, or dropped.

This project could not have become a reality without the support and cooperation of the institution's Superintendent, Coates Stuckey, and his staff. We also wish to thank the Hospital Improvement Program clerical staff who typed and collated the many rough drafts of this manual.

A Review of Behavior Shaping Through the Use of Reward Training

Reward training is a way of encouraging people to behave or act on their own. It is a positive way to teach retarded or normal individuals to behave or act in a desired way. It is generally agreed that most behavior is learned, and that the way a person behaves or acts is a result of what happens to him. What happens following an act or behavior is called the "reinforcement." The reinforcement may or may not be enjoyable and it may or may not satisfy a felt need. In reward training, a positive reinforcement is provided — one that is enjoyable or satisfies a need. The reinforcement is enjoyable to the degree that the child repeats the behavior that resulted in the reward. Thus, there is a "contingency" or contract to receive the pleasure; the child must do something to get the reward. The reward increases and strengthens the behavior or activity that has just occurred.

This contingent reinforcement procedure is a powerful training tool. In order to teach a new behavior, reward the child every time he accomplishes the desired behavior. This is called a continuous reinforcement. But after he acts as if he understands the contract (contingency) to maintain the desired behavior, reward the child for the acceptable behavior only at times (interval reinforcement). This is because a person does something for the desire of a reward. Once a person is satisfied (satiated) with the reward, there is no longer a desire for the reward, nor interest in working for the reward.

For the profoundly retarded person, reward training must be used with the technique of shaping. "Shaping" is taking an existing behavior and molding it into a more complex desired behavior. This goal is accomplished in small steps, making each step the best guess or approximation of the complex desired behavior. When this technique is used, a reward is given only for an acceptable approximation or an ABC (acceptable behavior change).

Shaping is very successful in moving a child from an undesirable behavior to a desirable behavior. Sometimes a behavior is desirable under certain conditions, but not desirable under a different set of conditions. For example, it is acceptable for a person to undress to take a shower, but it is not desirable to undress on the main street of town. The conditions determine when a behavior is desirable and to be rewarded or when it is undesirable and there will be no reward.

Remember to reward each time for a new desirable behavior, but also to give rewards at variable times for learned, established behavior. It is necessary to chain one step to another when using shaping procedures. "Fade out" or give fewer rewards as the new behavior is established.

It is very important to have the profoundly retarded child under behavior control before you begin teaching specific skills. "Behavior control" means that he attends to you, listens to you, and moves on command from you or the reward that you represent. Attending behavior should be well established before beginning communication shaping.

Giving rewards is not always easy. Sometimes it is difficult to provide the reward immediately; therefore, a "bridging signal" must be developed during training.

A bridging signal is usually a word such as "good," or a smile that tells the child that the reward is on its way. Remember that it is the desire for the reward that brings about the behavior. Be careful or stingy with rewards. Rewards are stronger or weaker at different times; for example, food is usually strong before lunch, but a toy may be desired after lunch. It is important to learn what turns your child on. What does he like? What is he willing to work for? Observe your child and see what takes place after he performs a behavior.

By using these reward techniques, together with the language activities described in the forthcoming chapters, you can begin a communication shaping program for your profoundly retarded child.

As you proceed to each of the developmental steps of communication and language, determine the ABC for that step. Using reward training techniques, develop the ABC completely before proceeding to the next ABC.

To fully understand reward training techniques, it is suggested you read Bensberg (1965), Watson (1969), Larsen and Bricker (1968), and Thompson and Grabowski (1972). You should also view the film *Teaching the Mentally Retarded: A Positive Approach.*

All of the language activities described in this book were done with the use of reward training techniques. It is important that you utilize these techniques throughout your communication shaping program. Before attempting language development, you should practice reward training techniques. A step-by-step practice set has been included to aid you. Post it nearby and use it.

CHAPTER GUIDE

Reward Training

You may practice reward training by either using a child or through role playing. If you are new at reward training, role playing is a good way to start.

Step 1 — Find out what your child likes.
       Does he like to be touched?
       What kind of food rewards does he like?

How much reward does it take to make him respond?
(These questions can be answered through observation
or by trial and error.)

Step 2 — Decide what the child can do now.

Observe him and give him several trials at a desired task
to determine his level of ability.
What do you want him to learn?

Step 3 — Get the child under behavior control.

Call the child by name and motion to him. Reach your hand
toward the child, then draw your hand back toward your face. This
means to pay attention to you: to look at you, eye to eye. If he
attends to your action, reward him. Do this many times, rewarding
only the desired response. After many trials, begin to reward only
every now and then when he attends.

Once he pays attention to you, teach him to come to you. Use
the three steps to teach the child "come to me." Reward him for any
movement toward you. Reward him every time until this behavior is
fully established.

Always call the child's name first. Train him to sit, then to
stand, then move from one chair to another, then to chairs further
apart. Keep developing behavior control until you are very sure
you have the child's attention and he will come to you from any
place or situation within your cottage, house, or training area,
when you say, "Tommy, come to me."

Step 4 — Teach him a skill.

Choose a task in which the child is to be trained or determine
the next ABC that is needed; for example, taking off pants. Break
the task into small parts. Train the child in each small part, always
going back to the previously learned part.

Practice constantly, and always be sure that the child is paying
attention and that you are rewarding properly.

2

What Is Communication?

Communication is an exchange of ideas and information. Ideas and information can tell about how you feel, what you want, or what you don't want. You can tell how a child feels, or what he wants, without hearing him say a single word. You can tell by the expression on his face, or because he cries. A child can tell you what he wants by pointing or reaching, or by nodding his head to say "yes" if someone helps him find what he wants. He can tell you what he doesn't want by pushing it away or screaming.

You can tell how someone else feels by looking at the expression on his face or seeing the droop in energy. You can learn what hurts by touching and getting a look of pain or being pushed away. Anyone working with children gets the idea quickly when a child grabs himself. You know it is time to rush him to the toilet!

All this is communication; an exchange of ideas without using words. It is an exchange by expression and by gestures. This kind of exchange of ideas is carried out mainly by seeing an expression on a face, a movement of a hand, or a nod of a head. You don't need to speak English or German or Spanish or Chinese to exchange ideas this way. Of course, there is a limit to how much can be communicated in this manner.

Using sounds that can be heard by someone else is another way to exchange ideas. Animals communicate this way; they make a variety of sounds. But an animal can only tell what is going on while it is going on — it cannot tell you what happened yesterday or what will happen tomorrow.

More than sounds, gestures, and looks are needed to tell what happened yesterday or any other time but right now, or to tell about plans, hopes, and wishes. Human beings are able to exchange ideas and information because they use a *system of symbols* — sounds that stand for a particular object or an idea that another human being can understand even without the object or idea being visible. These special sounds are symbols; they stand for the things and ideas that may not be present. These symbols are words. Humans have created a system for making sounds into words that tell what is needed, what is wanted, what has happened, what will happen. Words can explain any idea or give information. People who use the same system of symbols — the same language — can understand anyone else using that system of symbols.

When a person hears sounds or words that have meaning to him, or sees gestures or reads words, he is receiving ideas. This is called *reception,* or *receptive language.* Ideas can be received from another person by seeing and by hearing. Ideas can also be received by touching (blind people do this when they read braille).

When a person makes gestures or makes an expression with his face or uses words either by speaking or writing, it is called *expression,* or *expressive language.*

People also have a system of making a record of these symbols. This record is what we call writing. When a person can receive the ideas from the recorded symbols, that is called reading.

To communicate an idea to another person, it must first have some meaning inside the brain. An idea can be as simple as a feeling of hunger or sickness, a need, a like or dislike, a fear, or a pleasant experience. These ideas are called *inner language.*

If a child knows when he is hungry, when he needs to go to the bathroom, or is afraid he will fall, he has some inner language.

6

When he knows, without hearing or saying words, that something he sees or smells is good to eat, or that a chair is to sit upon or that shoes go on feet, some inner language is working. A child must have some inner language in order to communicate with others.

EARLY COMMUNICATION EXPERIENCES

A baby hears sounds around him and learns to attach meaning to these sounds. He reacts: gives back his feelings about these sounds by crying, screaming, smiling, or wiggling with joy.

When a sound has a definite meaning to a child, it is filed away in the brain and the child can make use of this meaning if he needs to. A sound can be pleasant, like cooing, humming, or gentle laughter; it could be the sound of friendly footsteps; or it could be a very unpleasant sound, like cross words, yelling, door slamming, or crying. All these sounds are learned without effort by most children because of the feelings of pleasure, happiness, discomfort, or even pain associated with them.

Babies make feeding sounds — sucking noises, clucking and smacking — and they hear the sounds they make. Soon it becomes fun to hear themselves make these sounds, and then babies will play with making noises. They blow bubbles of saliva and have fun wiggling their tongues and making a variety of sounds.

Deaf babies make all these noises up to about six months of age. Because they cannot hear themselves or anyone else, they stop cooing and stop making sounds except for crying. Babies must hear to keep on playing with sounds. At about ten to twelve months of age, a baby will make some sounds that have meaning to someone else who is listening — very likely "mama." Mama is thrilled. Her excitement and joy please the baby, so he says "mama" again, more excitement is created, and the sound becomes a word, a symbol for the nice lady who feeds him and loves him. Most babies all over the world say "mama" first, and they say "papa" very much the same way. These are really sounds with which a baby is playing. He learns to attach meaning to the sound when he makes a connection between the sound and the person sharing the sound — either "mama" or "papa." Of course, many babies say other words first.

7

If no one is around to be mama and to be excited and thrilled by the "mama" sound, the baby does not have a chance to learn that he has made a sound with special meaning. This is why babies in hospitals do not start to talk until much later.

Something else beside deafness or not having a mama to listen can keep babies from learning from the sounds around them. Some children have injuries to their brains that keep them from making the connection between the sounds that go in the ears and what the sound means when it reaches the brain.

These brain-injured babies have trouble storing up the meanings of sounds. Because they do not learn the differences between sounds — this sound is safe, this sound is good, that sound is pleasant — they become afraid of all sounds and scream with fear at noises that do not bother other children. They will put their hands over their ears to shut out all sounds. Many of these children can learn to attach meaning to sounds and therefore overcome this fear. It is not easy to teach these children to attach meaning to sound, but it can be done in many cases.

A large storehouse of meaningful sounds must be filed in the brain. This is done through experience and opportunities to play with sounds and attach meaning to them. This is what is done in a communication training program. Each child is provided with experiences and chances to build a storehouse of ideas. Having this storehouse of ideas is like a savings account from which ideas can be withdrawn when needed.

The machinery for speech is very complicated. When you say, "The big white dog ran around the field," can you keep track of what your tongue did? What your lips and jaw did? Did you remember breathing? Did you know your soft palate kept the air from going out of your nose? You really did not think about these things; they just happened when you decided to say something.

What would your speech be like if it did not happen just this way? You might stutter. You might not be able to say *r* or *s* or *th*. Your tongue might move so slowly that the sounds would run together. If you had a cleft or slow-moving palate, the air would go out through your nose instead of being controlled in your mouth to make the sounds you plan on. It is hard for children with these handicaps to learn to talk.

In order to talk, a child must have some need to talk. He must have ideas he wants to communicate and he must be physically able to communicate them. Sometimes, the parts of the brain where ideas are stored for use is injured so badly that the ideas just are not there. However, most children who move around, see, hear, or throw things have some ideas, however limited.

Some children are hushed up, or hear "sh" so often they are afraid to make sounds. Some children have so much done for them they do not need to try to talk; and some children do not have anything done for them and are not talked to at all so that they think they should not talk either.

The following summarizes the reasons children do not talk.

Deafness. The deaf children with good intelligence will struggle to get ideas out. The deaf child who is brain-injured and has retarded development may struggle to get ideas out but has trouble finding ways and may stop trying.

Brain injury. Brain injuries can make it difficult to attach meaning to sounds. The brain-injured child cannot receive meaning from sound, so he cannot store up any meanings and he has difficulty getting ideas out from his very poor storehouse of ideas.

Difficulty in using tongue, lips, jaw, etc. Down's Syndrome children often have this trouble. Heavy droolers often have some paralysis in the tongue muscles. These children have trouble making their tongues and lips behave for forming sounds for words.

The need to talk. The value of talking may not be understood because of bad examples, too much or too little attention, too much noise, or too much "sh-ing."

Most children will struggle to get some ideas across in one way or another. But some just stop trying. It could be said that the child who quits easily has failed so many times he just will not try anymore. Or he has met with impatience or punishment and has decided to keep quiet to keep the peace.

Communication develops in a pattern. This pattern is called a sequence. Most, but not all, children follow a sequence for developing language. Some will go much slower than others. Some will jump ahead quickly. Children learn through imitation. They need many opportunities to imitate their teachers and peers. When a child is led along the sequence in developing communication, he requires many experiences; chances to learn to listen and to attach meaning to gestures, movement, and sound. When a child has had many of these experiences — good watching, good listening, and meaningful movements — the chances are that he will begin to make appropriate responses.

An appropriate response (AR) is not necessarily words, in the beginning. When you get an AR to something you have helped a child do, you know he has attached meaning to the directions you gave him and he is reacting appropriately. When you say "Come to me, Tommy," holding out your hands, inviting him with a smile on your face, Tommy comes to you. He gives you an AR to what he sees (your smile and your hands), and what he hears ("Come to me."). He might also suspect a reward is waiting for him.

Later on, work to get an AR just through what the child hears. However, some children may always need a cue from a gesture to get the idea started.

On page 88 of this book is a chart of how most normal children follow the developmental sequence for communication. The children you are working with have not been moving steadily along this schedule for one or more of the reasons already mentioned. Following the chart are several forms to be completed to help you evaluate your children in terms of where they are in the developmental sequence for communication. It may take a child a long time to progress from one development to the next, but do not lose heart. Two years of learning to listen may seem like a long time, but it really pays off.

Here are some ideas to help your children learn to communicate.

1. Language is an exchange of feelings and ideas. This means two or more human beings are busy doing something together.
2. Always start each lesson time expecting to have fun and to enjoy each other.

3. Greet each child with a smile and an extended hand. Touch him warmly. Let him know you like to be with him.
4. Sing his name and play the little game "Is Tommy here?" or "Where is Tommy?" This game is explained in detail in Chapter 6.
5. Don't use too many words. A single word gently spoken, a smile, and a good gesture is much better than a long phrase or sentence.
6. Reread the sequence of language development occasionally to remind yourself of the order in which language develops.

As the meanings of experiences and ideas are stored in a child's brain for future use, inner language is developing.

Receptive Language is receiving ideas from experiences. This means the ideas we get:

from what is *heard;* noises such as bells, buzzers that mean special things, and words. Rhythms that mean "do something special" such as run, step, hurry, march, tiptoe. Music that tells something. Directions to do something such as "Come to me," "Sit down," "Stand up," "Stop," "Wait," "Don't touch," "No, not funny."

from what is *seen;* like a smile, frown, gesture, posture, pointing, threatening hand, welcoming hand, a nod "yes" or "no," signs, pictures, and printed words.

from what is *touched;* like texture — soft, hard, rough, smooth, sticky, slippery, hot, cold, wet, dry, chewy, liquid.

Learning from what is heard, seen, or touched starts with learning to pay attention to whatever you want the child to listen to, to look at, or to touch. This is prelistening training.

CHAPTER GUIDE

Prelistening Training

Step 1 — Tell someone what communication is.

Step 2 — What are the different ways of communicating? Demonstrate this to someone.

Step 3 — Prove to yourself through demonstration that someone is receiving your message.

Step 4 — Study the developmental scale for language levels. Check it by observing children in your neighborhood.

Step 5 — Do the children around you have a need to talk or communicate? Show yourself or somebody else how you know they have this need.

Step 6 — List several reasons why some children do not talk.

Step 7 — Practice listening to others. Practice watching others. Make a list of what your child is saying to you without words. Make a list of ideas you get from what you hear, ideas you get from things you see, ideas you get from things you touch.

3

Gaining a Child's Attention

Unless a child's attention is captured, no learning will take place. As you become familiar with behavior shaping techniques, you will find that you are capturing attention by using your hands, smiles, and rewards. In reward training, it is necessary to have the child under your behavior control before you try to train for a specific skill. The same is true for communication shaping; you must be able to capture the attention of the child before proceeding to develop communication skills.

Spend time watching your child, observing what he likes, what he is willing to work for, and what he attends to. Then you can use these things for rewards and for capturing the child's attention. The strength of the reward may be different at times. For example, some children like ice cream while others do not. But even the child who likes ice cream may not be willing to work for it right after lunch. Be prepared to use a variety of attention-getting items. If one thing does not work, try something else, and if that does not work, try again. You will find something that will work. Even the most profoundly retarded can learn to pay attention to you.

Using your hands in pleasant gestures, your smiles, and your rewards, you can shape communication. But we will add some new ideas to help capture attention.

The place where you will work should not be cluttered. Toys, games, objects, pictures, and gadgets should be out of sight. Only the one thing you are going to work with first should be available. This way only one thing will draw the child's attention. These children are easily frustrated when given a toy they are unable to use. A good test of whether or not a toy is right for a child is to watch carefully his interest in it. If he throws it on the floor or brushes it away, he is trying to tell you, "I don't know what to do, or how to do anything with this." Maybe you can show him how to play with it, but don't expect him to try if the toy is not within his interest range or is too hard for him to manage with his hands and eyes. Always have only one toy in front of the child to capture his attention. If he still wants to brush the toy aside, maybe it is too hard for him to manage, so put it away and get something he can handle.

Your voice and choice of words are very important. Speak gently and kindly, trying to use very few words. You do not need to sound cross just because you say only one word. You can say "look," "listen," "walk," "step up," and make these activities sound exciting and fun to do.

If you are helping a child learn to identify an object, use very few words (See Chapter 6). Let's say you are trying to teach him to understand that the word-sound "bed" means that thing over there that he sleeps on. The one word-sound you want him to pay attention to is "bed," so don't mix him up with a lot of words like "Now, Benny, I want you to show me your bed." Just take his hand gently, point to the bed, and say "bed, bed," very pleasantly. After you have given him a few words like this, "bed," "window," "potty," you can make a phrase such as "This is a bed," and later you can say "Show me your bed," or "Where is the window?"

When you start to work with a child, the very first moment you meet, whether he comes to you or you go get him, your own smile and warm feelings toward him will do more to get the child to pay attention than anything else. Your hand held toward the child, plus a smile that says "I like you and I like to be with you" means more to that child than you can imagine. The child must be greeted in such a way that he feels wanted and worthwhile. You need eye-to-eye contact with the child to get his attention, and a warm smile and quiet manner are the easiest and best ways to get it.

Let's say you are going to have the child sit at a table to do tongue exercises and you are going to sit beside him. Put on a little act. Sing the child's name, "Ben-ny, where's Benny?" and look around as if you cannot find him. He will probably look up at you. Then smile, give him a little hug, and say "Ben-ny, sure, here's Benny, Benny's here." All children like to feel very special, wanted, and like to hear their own names. If you are frowning, cross, hurrying, or if you grab, you spoil the fun before you can even get started. Remember that the first moment you get near a child is very important and sets the tone for the way you and the child will work together.

After you and the child are settled beside each other, it may be difficult to focus his attention on the task you have planned to do. If you have carefully planned just what you are going to do and how to go about it, the child feels your security and authority.

It will be necessary to work alone with one child at the start of a new activity or task. This one-to-one situation makes the child feel very special and removes the distraction of having other children and people around. The child can learn to pay attention more easily, which is important in learning to listen and to communicate. After he has learned to pay attention, many tasks can be done in groups. Since it is rare that a trainer is assigned only one trainee, you must learn how to achieve a one-to-one situation while maintaining control over your group.

The first step in behavior modification or reward training is to get each trainee under your behavior control. Once this is achieved, you may wish to conduct one-to-one training with a student while your other students are participating in a group controlled activity. A group controlled activity could be sitting quietly, seat work activity, coloring, routine free play, or a routine activity. Control is usually maintained by a verbal reminder to the group or by looking at the group periodically. Through cooperation with other trainers you can agree to switch groups so that you may conduct one-to-one training while a large group (two or more small groups) activity is being conducted.

If it is very difficult to get a child to look at you or to watch your hands, you will need to work alone with him in a quiet room. Sit down beside him with rewards handy, and bring out a plastic hourglass with colored specks in it. Tap the table gently with it and say "Look," and turn the glass over so the specks move down through the center of the toy. Say "Look," gently, close to his ear and hold your hand toward the toy. Reward him if he turns his head or moves toward the toy. You may need to move the toy slowly toward his hand and help him touch it, rewarding him when he touches it. A plastic hourglass is the easiest to use because it does not break easily and children seem to like it very much. As soon as the child has learned to look at the glass, show him how to turn it over. Try not to say anything except "Look," and the child's name such as "Look, Benny."

Another good toy is a small, liquid-filled lucite ball with an object floating in it. Gently roll it in front of the child, always rewarding the instant any attention is paid to the toy. Hand puppets are very good attention-getters, especially very smiley little boy or girl puppets. You can make a puppet wave, "Hi, Benny" and do many funny little things like scratch its head, clap its hands, touch the child, and touch you.

Wind-up gadgets such as a dancing monkey, a walking dog, or a wing-flapping butterfly are excellent, but they break very easily and are difficult to repair. If you are working with a very gentle child, these gadgets are worth a try.

Gaining the child's attention is the first step toward helping him communicate with you and others. The suggestions in this chapter will help make the task easier.

CHAPTER GUIDE

Gaining the Child's Attention

Step 1 — Observe what your child likes. Make a list.

Step 2 — Make a list of what your child pays attention to.

Step 3 — Practice talking gently and kindly.

Step 4 — Practice developing rapport with many different children at different times.

Step 5 — Practice playing "Benny, where's Benny?"

Step 6 — Make a list of what happens when you present a plastic hourglass to a child with retarded development.

Step 7 — Practice using hand puppets to gain attention. Make your own hand puppet.

Step 8 — Make a list of other gadgets not listed in the manual that you have used successfully to gain attention of your child with retarded development.

4

Total Body Activity

Many children with retarded development have very poor ideas about their own bodies; they seem not to know about their feet, or how to move one foot on purpose. They seem clumsy and totter easily. They have trouble regaining their balance. Many children can move about but with very little control of what, where, and how they move. Some children run more easily than they walk.

It may seem strange to start a language program with a kind of physical education program. Total Body Activity (TBA) is one way to help the child learn to attach meaning to sound and to follow directions. The child will learn *what* he moves, *where* he moves, and *how* he moves.

Through TBA, a child can learn to respond to directions with his whole body in many ways. To help the child learn to communicate, TBA is integrated with other programs being operated simultaneously (though not always at the same session). These other programs include exercising the tongue, lips and jaw

(Chapter 5), and receiving and attaching meaning to the names of things, people, and activity (Chapter 6). TBA and learning the names of body parts can, of course, go on at the same time. The lessons to shape and gain control of the tongue, lips and jaw should be done in a special classroom while working with one child alone.

Receiving and attaching meaning to the names of things and people beyond the body image is best taught in a one-to-one situation. This will require cooperation with other trainers to conduct large group activities with the remainder of your group while you are conducting one-to-one training. The TBA room should have plenty of space for moving around so that the child can move from one area to another for each activity. Just moving away from an activity helps change a thought pattern and draws attention to the next chore. A large gym mat should be placed on the floor in a quiet area. This mat should be at least 4' by 6' and made of a material that can be kept clean, and should be one solid color.

On the other side of the room, preferably divided by screens or partitions, an obstacle course should be set up. At the beginning of the program, only two things are needed in this area. One is a large barrel placed sideways on a low rack so it is very stable and won't move, and the other is a large box about 3' square and about 2' deep. This box should be very sturdy. Later, more things will be added (balance beams, a trampolet, stairs, etc.).

At least ten minutes should be spent with each child daily in teaching total body activity. Work with only one child at a time; another child can watch if he really *will* watch. The child should be barefooted and comfortable in shorts and tee shirt. Gym shoes can be worn except for activity on the mat or balance beam.

TEACHING BODY IMAGE

Knowing about your body, knowing the names of parts of your body and how they all fit together, is called *body image*. Many children with retarded development draw very strange pictures when asked to make a picture of themselves. These children have no idea of a body image.

An image is developed by teaching the names and locations of body parts. In order to follow directions, the child must know what to move in response to your spoken direction. If you say "Give me your hand" or "Put your foot in your pants," the child must know what the word "hand' or "foot" means in relation to himself. This portion of the TBA program, learning about body parts, is called *What We Move.*

The child must be taught the names of his own hands, arms, feet, legs, knees, head, tummy, and bottom. Learning these names is very important as the basis for a language program. These sound symbols are taught first because the child's own body can feel pressure on the part and he can connect the sound of the word with the part being touched. This tells the child what he moves so he can go on to learn the second part of the program, *Where We Move.*

"Where" is the direction we move: in, out, up, down, over, under, in front of, behind, and around. To move where we want to move requires control of the body, balance and an idea of direction.

Gravity is the force that pulls everything toward the center of the earth. When a baby learns to hold his head up, he learns his first lesson in controlling his head against the force of gravity. His neck muscles tighten up to hold his head steady against gravity, otherwise it would flop around. (This is evident in severely damaged children.) When the child sits up and stands, he has learned to control his muscles to hold his entire body up against gravity.

People have tiny stabilizers built into their heads near their ears. This is where good balance comes from. If you are dizzy, these stabilizers are not working right. In brain-damaged people, sometimes the muscles do not respond properly to stabilizing messages and balance is poor. Balance is natural for most people, but some children must learn to regain balance if they lose it for even a second. Balance is important in controlling where a child moves. When the child knows *what* he moves and *where* he moves, he is ready to learn *how he moves.*

"How" means learning to crawl, roll, walk, jump, swing, climb, turn, dive, tiptoe, slide, skip, run fast or slow, start, stop, stop quickly, and all combinations of these.

Teaching What We Move

You will need a soft 1″ wide paint brush, or you can make a whirly bird brush that is fun to use and helps get the child's attention. To make a whirly bird, obtain a battery-driven drink mixer. Remove the "swizzle stick." Cut off the handle of a soft camel's hair artist brush (about ½″ around) so that it is about 5″ long. Insert the handle of the brush where the mixer was removed. When the switch is turned on, the brush will whirl gently in a very small circle. When you touch a child's hand with the whirly bird or stroke the side of his arm or leg, it is a very pleasant feeling.

Mat Work. Work on a mat on the floor to help the child learn to find the parts of his body. Have the child lie down on the mat, kneel beside him, and play with him a little.

Pick up a hand and say "Hand." Rub his hand gently on the mat saying "Hand," pat his hand, stroke his hand, and say "Hand." Show him the whirly bird; let him touch it so that he's not afraid of it. Gently touch his hand with the whirly bird and say "Hand." Lift his hand each time you brush it and say "Hand." When he begins to move his hand as he hears the word "Hand" or sees the brush, reward him. Do the same thing with the other hand. Do not move from one part of the body to another too fast.

Do the same thing with one foot and then the other foot. When the child seems able to locate his hand or his foot when he hears the sound of the word, he is ready to try another activity, called "angel in the snow." This is teaching the child to move his arms from the sides of his body up the mat as far above the head as possible, and spreading his legs far apart. As you move the child's hand and arm along the mat say "Hand *out.*" Use the brush in one hand and hold the child's hand in your other hand. Return the child's hand to his side while saying, "Hand *in,*" and move his arm back to the side of his body. Use the brush on the *inner* side of the arm so that he knows what muscle must be used to move his arm. *Do not push the arm or shove it with the brush.* If the child needs help to move his hand, place your hand over the child's hand with your thumb on one side and your fingers on the other side. Use very light pressure and be sure it is equal from your hand to both sides of the child's hand.

Many sessions will be needed for some children to learn what is expected of them. Remember to reward desired behavior quickly.

Now do the same thing with the child's legs, starting with his legs straight and together. Move one leg out sideways, holding the thigh with equal pressure on both sides as you move his leg out and saying "*Out,* foot, *Out.*" Do the same thing to the other leg. When you want the leg to move in, stroke the inner side of the thigh. When you want the leg to move out, stroke the outer side of his thigh. Do not push the leg or shove it with the brush. Reward each correct try.

When the child can move each leg when you say "*Out,*" and can move both legs at the same time, out and in, work to get him to move his arms and legs at the same time. Say "Out," and "In," and move the brush around to let him find and know the muscles that are being used. Once in a while touch his tummy playfully with the brush, saying, "Tummy." This is usually a lot of fun.

During each lesson on the mat, be sure to name the part, stroke the needed muscles with the brush, and move the part first yourself while naming it again. Brush it again and keep trying to get the child to move by himself as you name the part. At first, remember to reward after each effort. Then, after you are sure the child can do what you have asked him to do, reward him only once in a while.

Never use the brush or whirly bird as a prod. If you want the arm and hand to move away from the body, stroke the muscles that will pull it away from the body. That means the outside of the upper arm and the shoulders. Brushing on the pulling muscles tells the child what muscles to use to help move his arm and hand where you want him to move it. You must touch the muscle you want to do the pulling. Never push with the brush. You may need to move the entire arm or leg to let the child get the feeling of what you want him to do.

Each time you begin work on the mat, start with his hands. Brush the hand gently with the whirly bird or the brush and say, "Hand." Do the same thing each time you review. Repeat what you have been doing, at the same time naming the body part you are working on. Always be sure to touch the body part after you have named it. Naming comes first, then stroking on the muscles that are going to move a body part.

Rolling over. Some children will roll over leading with their shoulders and dragging the rest of their body over; others will throw their hips over and drag the rest of their body. Let the child watch you roll over or watch some child who can already do it.

With the child on the mat, tell him to "roll over." He will likely decide what to try to move first, his shoulders or his hips. Reward him for any move, then help him move a little more and reward him again.

Some children are afraid to lie face down, yet it seems a little easier to roll over from face down to face up. If the child is afraid or unhappy lying face down, start him on his back. If he moves a shoulder first, take his arm and help him swing it over to pull his shoulder along. You can give him a little help by pushing his hips over after he has moved his shoulder. If he chooses to move his hips first, help him by swinging his leg over for him then pushing his shoulders over. Be sure to reward for the slightest move in the right direction. Remember to name the parts being touched or used, and say "Roll over," or "Roll back," whichever you are trying to get him to do.

Curling up in a ball. Start by pulling the child's knees up to his tummy as he is lying on the mat. This can be done with him on his back or lying on his side. Say "Curl up like a kitty," or "Stretch out like a big cat." Encourage the stretch, as this is a good activity. Help the child curl up in other ways. If a child does not seem able to do this even with planned shaping and rewards, go on to another activity. Come back and try it again another time.

Teaching Where We Move

The first task is to help the child understand the words "in" and "out." He has heard the words while moving his hands and feet on the mat. If the child is not afraid of the barrel, this is the easiest way to teach the idea of "in" and "out." If the child crawls in the barrel he can only go out; there is no other place to go. You can add the word "through" at this time.

Teaching the Words for "Where"

Say the word "In," as a demonstrator crawls in the barrel and say "Out," as she comes out of the other end. The total body goes *in* and the total body comes *out*. Use rewards to gain the right response to getting in the barrel and coming out. Coming out is easier when using the barrel.

Show the child how to get *in* the box and *out* of the box. It is easier to get *in* the box and harder to get *out*. When these two activities are easily done, using the commands "In" and "Out," it's time to add a more difficult in-and-out task.

Use hoops at least 30″ in diameter, made of plastic water hose taped to make a loop. The plastic hoops bought at variety stores are too fragile and don't last very long. Place one of the hoops on the floor, take the child's hand and say, "Step in the hoop; step out of the hoop." You can continue by teaching him to sit *in* the hoop, to sit *beside* the hoop, to *pick up* the hoop, and to put it *down*.

Place one hoop on the backs of two chairs placed with their backs facing each other. Have the child crawl *under* the hoop saying, "Under you go." Have him step *into* the hoop saying, "In you go," and later have him step out of the hoop as you say, 'Out you go."

Use a 12′ rope, attached to the wall about 12″ above the floor. Have the rope lying on the floor and show the child how to step *over* the rope. When he does this easily, lift the free end of the rope so that the main part of the rope is about 3″ off the floor. Now teach him to step *over* the rope. When he easily steps *over*, raise the rope until it is about 18″ off the floor. Now teach him to go *under* the rope. Hold the free end so you can give him more room to crawl *under* if he needs it.

Later use a set barrier such as a board across two chairs to step or climb *under* or *over*.

Up and down are important words. Learning to step *up*, step *down*, and step over will be very helpful when going on walks or learning to use playground equipment. Arrange a sturdy box no more than 8″ high to teach the child to *step up* and *step down*. Later add practice stairs for *up* and *down*. Stairs should have banisters or railings, placed at two heights for the child to hold on to. Stairs without railings are much harder to use.

Use a bandana handkerchief with a knot tied in one corner, for a better grip. Swing the handkerchief around, up, and down. After the child can swing it around easily, you hold a handkerchief too. Sing "Swinging, swinging, here we go *up,*" and toss the hand holding the handkerchief up high as you say "up," loud and with a higher tone of voice. Then bend down, saying, "Here we go *down,*" dropping the hand holding the handkerchief to the floor. If the child imitates your action in the slightest way, reward him. Do this several times in a row.

Over and *under* can be taught with any barrier. The rope fastened to the wall is the best to start with because you can lower or raise the rope to gain an easy reward for the child. You can also have the child crawl *under* a table or two chairs placed to make an arch as you say, "Under you go." Do not try to use the caterpillar tunnels until the child is very comfortable and able to go under the table or two chairs.

Balance

Many severely handicapped children are clumsy because they have a poor sense of balance. If they lose their balance, they usually fall because it is hard for them to recover it. Training a child to balance is very important.

Straddling an 18″ cylinder such as a strong waste basket is good training. Hold the child's shoulders to steady him and gently rock him sideways so that he learns he can use his feet to steady himself and regain his balance.

A small trampolet ("Jumping Jiminy") is very good to use for a small child, but must be used with caution while an attendant holds the child's hand until the child learns to hold on to a bar or rail.

Thirty-six inch diameter inflated balls are excellent for teaching about balance. Hold the child as he lies on the ball, toes just touching the floor, and roll him up and then back down on his feet again. The children love it and they learn a lot about balance this way.

Walking a Balance Beam

Balance beams are rigid, sturdy boards placed at least 6″ off the floor. The beams for beginners are 6″ wide and 4′ long. This activity is a little frightening for the child, so it is best not to use a board that has any spring in it. At first work barefooted.

Some children will be able to start out working on the balance beams, while some will need to be taught to walk on a line on the floor first. Place a strip of brightly-colored tape, at least 4″ wide and about 10′ long, on the floor. Or paint a bright line on the floor. Walk on the line yourself and say, "Look, walk." Reach down and touch the line and say, "Line, look; line, walk." Reward the child as he looks at the line. Take the child's hand in yours and walk backwards, leading him along the line. Reward him for any attempt to walk the line. Later on, hold one hand only as you guide him. Eventually you will be able to just offer your hand and he will be able to walk the line. Always say, "Look, line, walk." Do not say anything else. You can also cut out footprints and paste them on the floor for the child to walk on.

Place a board on the floor; the same board that you will later use as a balance beam. Say, "Look, walk," and follow the same way of leading and helping the child to walk along the top of the board. Remember to reward at the right time, and for each new effort and success.

When this has been mastered, try the balance beam a few inches off the ground. If the child is afraid to get up on the beam, put the board back down on the floor until he gets braver. Do not try him on the raised board until he can walk the board on the floor comfortably. Graduate to a 4″ wide by 6′ long board.

Here is a list of exercises to do on the beams. Keep a record for each child, and move him to a more difficult task when he has mastered a simpler one.

EXERCISES USING A RIGID BALANCE BEAM[1]

1. Walk forward on beam, arms held out from sides.
2. Walk backward on beam, arms held out from sides.
3. Walk to the middle, turn around, walk backward; arms held out from side.
4. Walk forward to the middle of the beam, turn, continue sideward left with weight on the balls of feet.
5. Walk to center of beam, turn, and continue sideward right.
6. Walk forward, left foot always in front of right.
7. Walk forward, right foot always in front of left.
8. Walk backward, left foot always in front of right.
9. Walk backward, right foot always in front of left.
10. Walk forward, hands on hips.
11. Walk backward, hands on hips.
12. Walk forward, beanbag balanced on top of head.
13. Walk forward, pick up a beanbag from middle of beam.
14. Walk forward to center, kneel on one knee, rise, continue to end of beam.
15. Walk backward, beanbag balanced on top of head.
16. (Place beanbag at center of beam.) Walk to center, place beanbag on top of head, continue to end of beam.
17. (Have aides hold a wand 12″ above the center of the beam.) Walk forward on beam, step over wand.
18. Walk backward, step over wand.
19. (Have aides hold wand 3′ over beam.) Walk forward and pass under the wand.
20. Walk backward, pass under the wand.
21. Walk backward, hands clasped behind body.
22. Walk forward, arms held out from sides, palms down, with a beanbag on back of each hand.
23. Walk backward, arms held out from sides, palms down, with a beanbag on back of each hand.

---

[1] Some of these activities are adaptations of Kephart's (1960) Perceptual Motor Training Activities.

24. Hop on right foot, full length of beam.
25. Hop on left foot, full length of beam.
26. Hop on right foot full length of beam, turn, hop back.
27. Hop on left foot full length of beam, turn, hop back.
28. Walk to center, balance on one foot, turn on same foot, walk backwards to end of beam.
29. Walk to center, left sideward, turn, walk to end of beam right sideward.
30. With arms clasped about the body to the rear, walk forward.
31. With arms clasped about the body in rear, walk to center, turn, walk backward.
32. Walk backward with beanbag balanced on back of each hand.
33. Walk to center, do balance stand on one foot (arms held out from sides with trunk and free leg held horizontally).
34. (Hold wand 15″ above beam.) Balance beanbag on head, walk forward, step over wand.
35. (Hold wand 15″ above beam.) Balance beanbag on head, walk sideward right, step over wand.
36. (Hold wand 15″ above beam.) Balance beanbag on head, walk sideward left, step over wand.
37. (Hold wand 15″ above beam.) Balance beanbag on head, walk sideward right, step over wand.
38. (Hold wand 3′ above beam.) Walk forward, hands on hips, pass under bar.
39. (Hold wand 3′ above beam.) Walk backward, hands on hips, pass under bar.
40. Walk forward, eyes closed.
41. Walk sideward, eyes closed.
42. Walk backward, eyes closed.
43. Stand, feet side by side, eyes closed, record number of seconds balance is maintained.
44. Stand, one foot in advance of the other, eyes closed, record number of seconds balance is maintained.
45. Stand on right foot, eyes closed, record number of seconds balance is maintained.

46. Stand on left foot, eyes closed, record number of seconds balance is maintained.
47. Place hands on beam, have partner hold legs as in wheelbarrow race, walk to end of beam. (Partner straddles beam and walks on the ground.)
48. Place hands on beam, have partner hold legs as in wheelbarrow race, walk to end of beam. (Partner walks on beam.)
49. Walk on all fours (hands and feet on beam).

A 2″ x 4″ x 12′ board placed upon blocks to hold it about 6″ above the floor will be a little bouncy. This is not really a balance beam such as we have been talking about, but it is very good to help train the child to get control of balance. This is a fun activity and one that the child should learn to do very early. The springy board is not for all the tasks listed, but it's fun to use now and then.

Learning balance recovery helps the child control his body as he does things he is asked to do or things he wants to do.

Teaching How We Move

The ability to control and direct your body is called *motor planning.* Most of us motor plan without even thinking about it. Some children must be taught how to motor plan.

Some children run more easily than they walk and it's not always easy to slow them down to a walking speed. Walking hand in hand with an adult who is saying pleasantly, "Walk, walk, walk, walk, walk, walk," is a fun activity and attaches the word "walk" to the activity Add variety to walking by using music, drums, singing a song, or marching in a circle around the room while lifting knees high. A child can be taught to tiptoe or jump in place. Skipping is very hard to teach, and many severely handicapped children will not learn this rhythmic combination of hopping and walking.

Try playing follow-the-leader with one child. Have him imitate *how you move* as you walk, run, stop, march, or hurry. If you use good rhythm and keep saying, "Walk, walk, walk," or "Run, run, run," the child should imitate your action.

Getting a child to motor plan takes some thinking on his part. Some children seem unable to do this, but it's worth a try. Stand on one side of the mat and have the child stand on the other side. Say, "Come to me," holding your hands in his direction. As he moves toward you, always reward him. Go to the other side, face him, and say, "Come to me, run." When he can follow directions to "Come to me," as you say either "Walk," "Run," "March," "Crawl," "Roll," or "Hop," he is responding well to these words. The next step is to have him decide how he will come to you.

If he chooses to run the first time, say "Come to me, run!" You are teaching him that the word "walk" or "run" means the way he moved. When the child can come to you either way you call it, walking or running, you can add other ways to move toward you or toward someone or something that you name and he can understand.

As the child progresses in the TBA program, he is learning to listen and respond appropriately. When each body part can be identified, the names of body parts have become meaningful. The sound of the word means a definite thing. As the child responds appropriately to "in," "out," etc., he has attached meaning to those words. This is the basic purpose of the TBA program: To use the child's own body and its movements to learn to attach meaning to spoken words.

After a year of daily sessions with the TBA program, the aides working with the experimental group recorded the following observations: "The children seem much less clumsy." "They move better and walk straighter." "Response to verbal directions is very good." "They follow directions when given with a very few well chosen words."

"It is much easier to take the children out for walks. They don't stumble along. They can step *up* or *down* a curb. They can step *over* a puddle or something that might make them trip or stumble. When they walk to the canteen (and this they couldn't do with any ease or control before), they all walk *up* and *down* the stairs with no hand rails; most of them had had to be helped or almost dragged or carried *up* and *down* the steps. They go up the stairs when you tell them to."

31

"Several of the children now respond to 'Go play' on the playground and use some of the equipment such as the swings and climbing bars."

While interviewing aides about this phase of the program, it became apparent that a few verbal directions were being used without gestures: "Brush your teeth," "Go take a bath," "Go get your shoes (pants, any article of clothing)." "Touch your ——— (head, leg, arm, tummy, nose, teeth, mouth, tongue)," "Go to the bathroom." No effort had been made to explore the responses without accompanying gestures. The use of gestures is so deeply entrenched in the aide's function that it would be very difficult to do this. The essential point is that the children followed directions much better than they did before the program was started. Observation of the gestures used by the aides indicates that the gestures are very simple and barely significant. General directions for movement, such as supine hands (with palms up) for "up," "come to me," "step up," "step over," "pull it up," and pronated hands (with palms down) for "down," "sit down," "pull it down," and "step down," accompanied the verbal direction.

CHAPTER GUIDE

Total Body Activity

I. Learning "what we move" activities.

 Step 1 — Child should be barefooted, wearing shorts and tee-shirt.

 Step 2 — Use a soft brush or "whirly bird."

 Step 3 — Mat work.

 A. Pick up hand, say "Hand," rub hand gently on mat, pat hand, stroke hand.

 B. Reward whenever he moves his hand after he hears the word "hand."

 C. Repeat with other hand.

 D. Repeat with foot.

 E. Repeat with other foot.

 F. "Angel in the Snow" activity.

   G. Naming comes first, moving comes second.
   H. Rolling over.
   I. Curling up in a ball.
 II. Learning "where we move" activities.
   Step 1 — In-and-out activities.
   Step 2 — Inside-and-outside activities.
   Step 3 — Up-and-down activities.
   Step 4 — Trampolet activities.
   Step 5 — Over-and-under activities.
   Step 6 — Walk the line.
   Step 7 — Balance beam.
 III. Learning "how we move" activities.
   Step 1 — Walk hand in hand.
   Step 2 — Walk to music.
   Step 3 — Follow the leader.
   Step 4 — Run together.
   Step 5 — Hop together.
   Step 6 — Starting and stopping movement.

5

Tongue, Lip
and Jaw Exercises

Most children need help to improve the use of their lips, tongue, and jaw. The proper functioning of these parts of the body is necessary in developing communication.

All tongue, lip, and jaw exercises should be limited to five or ten minute sessions. It is better to have several short sessions rather than one long one. If the child tires very rapidly, shorten the lesson time. A good order of training is as follows:

1. Move tongue in and out of the mouth.
2. Move tongue from one corner of the mouth to the other.
3. Move tongue tip to upper lip and teeth.
4. Move tongue to lower lip and teeth.
5. Move lip, starting with large movements and developing small movements.
6. Change from tongue movement outside the mouth to tongue movement inside the mouth.

LIP EXERCISES

The easiest lip exercise is blowing, which also helps the tongue. Seat the child comfortably next to you, with a large mirror in front of both of you. Point to your lips and say, "Look." Blow brightly colored paper bits on the table or a feather on a string. Ask the child to try it by saying, "Blow" and moving the material close to his mouth. If the child cannot blow, let him watch you blow and allow him to play with the material. Most children can learn to blow with a little experience.

Other blowing games include blowing strips of kleenex or tissue, blowing a horn or whistle, blowing a ping pong ball on a table, blowing bubbles in water with a short straw, and blowing party favors. Party favors that can be seen and felt, such as those that have colored feathers or roll out as you blow, often work best with the child. Blow the favor first, then encourage the child to try to blow it.

Another good lip exercise is puckering or blowing kisses. Have the child imitate you. Sticky candy rubbed on the lips encourages lip action to remove it. You may have to move the child's lips with your fingers if he cannot move them by himself.

TONGUE AND JAW EXERCISES

The child should be able to move his tongue with some control. If he cannot lick an ice cream cone or suck through a straw, you will have to teach him. The child should be able to move the end of the tongue in and out of the mouth, from one corner of the mouth to the other corner, and move the tip of his tongue to the roof of his mouth. He should be able to move his tongue without moving his head.

A clear lucite shield, ½" thick, 24" wide, and 18" high, held upright on a slotted wooden base can be used for tongue exercises. A 2" wide oval is cut in the shield so the child can stick his tongue through it. Set the shield on a table with the child seated on a chair in front of the table. Hold a food reward on the opposite side of the shield and have the child stick his tongue through to try to reach the reward. Candy and food can be put on the sides of the hole, with the child attempting to lick the food off without turning his head. You may have to hold the child's head steady. By moving the food around the hole, you can have the child move his tongue to the side, up, and down. Clean the shield with a disinfectant after each use.

When teaching tongue exercises, use something you know the child likes well and is sticky so it can be felt and tasted. Lollipops, cake frosting, sticky candy, or peanut butter on a spoon work very well.

Hold the food near the child's tongue so he can lick it. If he cannot move his tongue, put the food on it so he can taste the food for a reward. Let the child work to lick the food. Slowly move it away so he has to move his tongue to taste it. You may have to move his tongue with the spoon or lollipop. You may also have to move your own tongue to show the child how to do it.

Put some food on the center of the child's lip and in the corner of his mouth and let him try to get it with his tongue. Reward him with a smile or a hug as soon as success is noted.

When the child can move his tongue on the outside of his mouth, use the same techniques to teach movement on the inside. Sticky food can be put on the inside lip corners and behind the upper teeth to encourage tongue movement. Up-and-down tongue movement is often the hardest to obtain, but don't be discouraged. It may take weeks.

Any kind of chewing is a good tongue exercise, so coarse foods should be encouraged. This also develops jaw muscles and encourages swallowing control. The food will serve as the reward.

Sucking through a short plastic straw is good exercise and can be fun. Give the child kool-aid or soda, or use other colored good-tasting liquids as a reward. Take a hard plastic straw and cut it off a little bit shorter than the height of the glass. Fill the glass no more than three quarters full. Put the straw in the glass and turn the glass up and let the child drink on the side of the glass with the straw. As he drinks out of the glass and straw, move the straw up with your finger until the child is drinking out of the straw alone and the glass is in an upright position. The child will suddenly discover that he is drinking through a straw.

Another way to teach drinking through a straw is to pipe the liquid up the straw by putting the straw in the liquid and putting your finger over the top of the straw. You can then lift the straw from the glass and keep the liquid in it. Put one end of the straw in the child's mouth and tip up the straw so the child will get the liquid when you remove your finger. As the child gets the idea of drinking from the straw, slowly transfer his straw to the glass.

A fun game is to have the child imitate your tongue movements in front of a mirror. Seat the child and yourself in front of a large mirror. Point to your tongue and move it side to side or up and down. Point to his tongue and say, "You do it." Both of you do it in front of the mirror. Practice smiling and watch the tongue pull in.

The child should be trained to hold his tongue in his mouth and not allow it to hang out. This improves his appearance and reduces drooling. The exercises described should provide enough control so the child can do this. These exercises also improve the child's ability to chew and swallow food and take medication orally.

The tongue, lip, and jaw exercises should be continued until the child can chew, swallow, suck through a straw, keep his tongue in his mouth, drool less, and has enough voluntary control over his tongue, lips, and jaw to make some speech sounds. When the child stops making progress, ask yourself why this has happened. Do you need a new approach or new methods? If the child's speech mechanism has been improved as much as possible and the child is naming objects or using words spontaneously, the exercises can probably be reduced or stopped. Children who are still having some difficulty controlling their tongues, lips and jaws may need the exercises continued but less often to maintain their skills.

Remember that tongue and lip control is a slow process that is accomplished one step at a time. There are many rewards in it for both you and the child.

CHAPTER GUIDE

Tongue, Lip, and Jaw Exercises

   I. Lip exercises

A. Blowing
    1. use a mirror
    2. bright colored papers
    3. feathers
    4. ping pong ball
    5. strips of kleenex
    6. horn whistle
    7. bubbles
    8. party favors
B. Puckering
C. Blowing exercises
D. Using sticky candy

II. Tongue exercises
  A. Lick sticky food or ice cream
  B. Move tongue through a lucite shield
  C. Lick lollipop, cake frosting
  D. Lick off sticky food from center or corners of lips, from behind upper lip
  E. Exercise tongue inside mouth
  F. Chew
  G. Suck through a straw
  H. Imitate tongue movements

III. Jaw exercises:
  A. Chew
  B. Imitate aide

6

Attaching Meaning to Sound: Receptive Language

Learning to listen and learning to attach meaning to a word sound was started with the TBA program. The child learned to respond as he listened and heard the word sounds for parts of his body. He learned to move in response to directions such as "Come to me," "Pull," "Put on," "In," or "Out." He learned to respond to the word sounds for how to move, such as "Walk," "Run," "Roll over," or "Jump."

So many words now have meaning for the child. He listens to a direction such as "Step up" and responds appropriately. He can show you a foot or a knee or a hand when he hears the word spoken clearly. So far, he has been using his body to respond. This is the hear-and-do step in learning.

When you add gestures to the words you use in communicating with the child, he is responding to see-and-do as well as hear-and-do. Sometimes it is difficult to know how much of the response is imitative of what he sees and how much he shows he is attaching meaning to the words he hears. If his response is appropriate at a later date, without gestures, you can feel quite sure the word sound itself has meaning.

Learning to listen and to respond appropriately is a long, slow process. For the time being, you will be working to build up the child's inner language; the ideas which have meaning to him in his mind. You should not demand spoken language at this point. It is possible to obtain a spoken response (especially with Down's Syndrome children), but these responses are only mimicry. You are working toward the child's *use* of words as a meaningful exchange of ideas. Later, when inner language is well-developed, you will use behavior shaping techniques to help the child attach meaning to sounds and to make an appropriate response. This is called *Identifying*. When spoken words are used, it is called *Labeling*.

In identifying, the child attaches the word he hears to the action or thing he sees. Labeling is saying the right word when he hears or sees action, or a thing or object. The final goal is to *use* words to exchange ideas.

TEACHING IDENTIFICATION

Use the big things in the child's world to attach meaning to word sounds, and use the child's own bed as a starter. Take the child's hand and lead him to his bed. Say to him as you pat the bed, "Bed — Bed." Use only the word "bed." Do the same thing with the window.

When you have done this several days in a row, using just two things at a time, begin to ask for identification. You say the word and expect the child to show you that he knows what that word means. Say "Bed — put your hand on your bed." Take his hand and gently help him to touch his bed if he doesn't do it by himself. Reward him the minute his hand touches his bed. If he only turns his head and looks toward his bed when you say "Bed," reward him quickly and reward him again as his hand touches his bed.

You can say "Put your hand on . . ." or "Show me." Always put the emphasis on the word you are teaching. Do not use any more words; you will just confuse him. The idea is to attach meaning to the one word you are working on.

Use just two objects at first. Decide which things are most likely to bring success. Continue to do this, adding things that are very familiar to him such as articles of clothing, a spoon, or a food tray.

Through the TBA program, the child has already attached meaning to the words for parts of the body, for directions, and for action. These programs should be operating at the same time, with the TBA program starting about two weeks before you begin identifying objects. In the TBA program, the child has been moved through this identifying level to a do-and-say level, where you actually ask for words such as "Jump — say jump."

Learning to listen is very important. It means just one thing: hearing a sound that means something. He learns that things have names. Teaching a retarded child to listen may take less than a year, or it may take a full year or longer. A great deal of patience is needed to help the retarded child through this learning-to-listen time.

When the child is experiencing success with identifying the large things in his world, start with smaller objects. Sit down at a table with the child beside you and a mirror in front of you. Do not have anything else on the table. A small, private room with just a table, mirror, necessary chairs, and a container for the objects to be used is a good place to work and avoid distractions. Have some attention-getters handy, such as an hourglass and some tree blocks.

At the start of each session play the game, "Is Tommy here?" (Use the child's own name.) Sing the question, "Is Tommy here?" and as you sing it two or three times, look everywhere except at the child whose name you are using. Slowly extend your upturned hand toward the child, look at him as if surprised, and say, "Yes, Tommy's here!" Smile, take his hand and place it in your hand, and again say, 'Yes, Tommy's here — hello, Tommy." Smile and pat his hand. If you are working with more than one child at a time, do the same thing with each child. You must be a real ham; the children love it and pay close attention just to get your smile and warm hand pat. Children with retarded development respond very well to this game; it seems to make each child feel special and worthwhile. Be sure to keep smiling and to look surprised at the right moment.

Teach a child to listen and to learn that different sounds mean different things by using noisemakers such as jingle bells, maracas, and rhythm sticks.

You can use a set of bells made for use in rhythm bands, a little circle of tape with bells fastened on it, or even an old fashioned dinner bell.

Maracas, or dried gourd rattles (or small plastic bottles with pebbles in them), can be bought at any music store. Rhythm sticks are just two ¾"-diameter dowels, 10" long. You can buy them at a music store or make them yourself.

Put a jingle bell on the table and then pick it up and shake it. Put it down again. Let him pick it up and shake it. Do this a few times, then put it out of sight.

Next, put the maracas or a rattle on the table, then shake it. Let him do it. Let him play with the maracas and the bell, picking them up one at a time and shaking them. Then take them away gently.

Get the child busy with some tree blocks or a toy. Shake the bell or rattle where he can't see it. When he looks around for it, stop, put a "Where is it?" expression on your face, and make the sound again. When he looks for the maracas or even turns his head a little bit, reward him, then give it to him whether he finds it or not. Stack up the tree blocks to get his attention back to the table and shake the bells again out of his sight. Do this a few times.

At the next lesson, be sure he is busy with some toy, then shake the bell out of sight. When he looks for it, show him both the bell and the maracas. He should reach for the one that made the noise. If he does not, offer him the right one and shake it for him. Do this until he can choose the right one. It may take many sessions to learn to do this. Don't be discouraged. Keep trying.

As he learns the difference between the bells and the maracas, change the maracas for a drumstick or rhythm stick. Go through the same procedure. Be sure he knows what is making the noise he hears. Then change the bell to a squeaky toy and add other things that make noise. Try to find a toy kitty that meows, a toy cow that moos, or a toy bird that cheeps. Using a whistle or a horn won't work, because he can see you. Use only two noisemakers at a time.

Trying to choose from three noises is too much at this point. This is a fun game and you should try it every day for a minute or two, even after it is learned.

After the child has become good at identifying noisemakers, introduce some common objects for him to identify. Use doll house furniture and such items as a toy bed, spoon, toy bus, cup, potty, or shoe.

Put the toy bed on the table, and with a gentle tap say "Bed" and smile. Now say "*Bed,* put your hand on the *bed*" (or "Show me the *bed*"). You will know which works better from earlier sessions moving around the cottage. Reward any move of his hand toward the right object. If the child makes no move, smile, take his hand gently, again say, "*Bed,* put your hand on the *bed*," and place his hand on the right object. Reward him.

Now put the toy bed out of sight in your lap or a handy drawer and place another object on the table, following the same steps. The spoon or potty would be good.

Bring out the bed again. Tap it on the table and say "Bed." Leave it there. Bring out the spoon. Tap it on the table and say "Spoon." Leave it there. Now say, "Tommy, put your hand on the bed." He must decide which object matches the word he hears. Smile. Reward any move toward the right object. Place his hand gently on the right object if he does not do it himself. Reward him.

Leave both objects on the table. Name them again as you pick each up and tap it down on the table again. Now say, "*Spoon,* put your hand on the *spoon.*" Follow the same method you used with the bed.

Do this a few times then put one object away and use another, keeping either one of the first two as an old friend. Always be pleasant and gentle and reward promptly. Ten minutes is enough time for one session.

After several sessions, the child should respond appropriately by *identifying* — picking out the correct object from the spoken word he hears you say. Keep changing the objects as success is noticed. When the child can select the right object each time, you can place three things on the table, following the same steps.

Some children will do better with pictures of objects. Some do better with selecting and identifying miniatures or small objects. If you use pictures, choose good color photographs of objects familiar to the child. The pictures should be mounted on sturdy cardboard. Include a photo of a favorite foster grandparent or aide. Always reward the child for each successful move toward identification. Gradually lessen rewards as the child succeeds.

Work up to eight objects or pictures. The following are good to use.

Ball
Bed
Bell
Bunny
Box
Bottle
Boat
Potty
Pillow
Blanket
Chair
Sock
Shoe
Spoon
Pants

Always start each lesson with an easy task you are sure he can do. End each lesson with an old friend; something he knows he can do. The child must have the feeling of success, even if you must help him a bit. Help him less as time goes on. Always speak gently and clearly. Never raise your voice or sound demanding. Yelling will just spoil the whole lesson time. It must be pleasant and happy and something he looks forward to.

When the child can identify these objects as you touch each one and you say its name for him first, try a harder step. Ask him to identify the right object just by hearing you say the word while all the objects are on the table. Do not touch the object first. His eyes can help if he sees you touch it. Use the same objects or pictures. Start with two, then move on to three to select from. Keep smiling and be sure to reward any move toward the right object or picture.

TEACHING LISTENING

When the child can easily identify the objects you have been working with, it is time to teach him the word "Listen." He must look right at you when you say, "Listen" and try hard to understand what you mean. It may be necessary to capture his attention when you say, "Listen," by gently taking his chin in your left hand, and slowly waving your right hand in front of his face until he looks at your hand. Then move your hand toward your lips as you say, "Listen: Ball, give me the ball." As you say the words, point to your mouth (but don't cover it). His eyes will follow your moving hand as you move it toward your mouth. As soon as you are sure he is looking at your mouth, say, "Listen: Ball, give me the ball." Always be gentle and smiling. Reward him as soon as you think he is looking at your mouth. The word "ball" is a good one to start on because he can see you say it.

The next step is to have the child listen to more than just the identifying words. When you say "Listen: Ball, give me the ball," extend your hand to receive it. Help him to succeed and reward him for any appropriate response.

Put a box on the table, saying, "Box" as you put it down. Show the ball to the child. Say, "Ball, listen: Put the ball in the box." Guide him with your hand until he gets the idea. Reward him as the ball goes into the box, with or without your help.

Do the same thing with several of the objects until each has been put in the box. Then take all the objects out of the box and put them out of sight. Select two of the objects and put them back on the table. Name one of them without touching it. Say, "Ball, listen: Ball, put the ball in the box." Help him if he needs it and reward him. Name the other object, "Spoon, listen: Spoon, give me the spoon." Help him if he needs it and reward him. Speak firmly but gently. Say the word "Listen" carefully and clearly.

Do this for several lessons until the child is good at selecting the right object and following the right directions. You can vary the directions after "in the box" or "give me" is understood. If you are working with a small group, you can say, "Spoon, listen: Spoon, give the spoon to Linda (or any child in the group)."

Start each lesson with a review, naming each article first and asking each child to do something you are sure he can do. Guide the child's hand away from making a mistake. He must get the feeling of success as he responds to the word "Listen." Reward him.

Music will capture the attention of children and can be used as a tool for learning. Use music and rhythm whenever possible. It is a joyful experience, except for the few children whose tolerance for music hinders rather than helps them learn. In some cases, music is more distracting than helpful.

BASIC WORD LISTS

These words have been selected because it has been shown that they are more easily learned, contain most of the sounds in a variety of combinations, are familiar, and are useful in general communication.

The communication shaping program started with children with profoundly retarded development, using the basic word list for a vocabulary. The traditional basic word list was usable and the children had some success in learning to use these words. However, the words that the children learned to understand and the words that came spontaneously made up another basic word list that the attendants felt was very important. These words are the real words the child understands and which get the appropriate responses necessary for communication in cottage life. This list consists of words the children understand and to which they give an appropriate response (AR). These are words that are important to daily living. The children heard them spoken and saw some gesture made by the attendant at the same time. Some of the words are understood without gestures, although it is seldom that an attendant speaks to a child without using some hand motion. There are three groups of words: those understood with gestures, those understood without gestures, and words spoken by the children and used appropriately.

Words Understood With Gestures

In watching the gestures used by the attendants, it appeared that the motion of the hands helped capture the child's attention more than it gave a clue for action. Many gestures were the same for several different commands, yet the children responded properly to each spoken word.

"Come to me"	"Walk"
"See it"	"Run"
"Stand up"	"Crawl"
"Sit down"	"Clap"
"Pull"	"Step up"
"No"	"Step over"
"Stop"	"Up"
"Let's go"	"Down"
"Get your partner"	"Go over"
"Go eat"	"Go under"
"Put on"	"Get in"
"Wait"	"Get out"
"Give it to me"	"Jump"
"Put it back"	"Turn"
"Put it in the dirty clothes"	"Turn around"
"Look"	"Wash your hands"
"Pile it up"	"Food"
"Listen"	

Many of these words were learned during TBA. This shows how important the TBA program is in making children aware that things and actions have names and labels.

Words Understood Without Gestures

This list of words bring an AR without gestures from the attendants.

"Brush your teeth"

"Bath" ("Go take a bath," "Now it's time for a bath")
"Go get your shoes (or any article of clothing)"
"Show me your hands (or feet, knee, eyes, ears, head,
    leg, arms, tummy, nose, teeth, mouth, tongue)"
"Go to the bathroom"

Added to this is a list of words sometimes responded to without gestures, but not by all the children.

"Go eat"	"Jump"
"Step up"	"Food"
"Step over"	"Wash your hands"

Words Spoken by Children

These are the words the children themselves use to communicate. These could be the target words in training sessions for learning to say and use words.

"Bus ride"	"Ice cream"
"Canteen"	"Pants"
"Water"	"Shoe"
"Bathroom"	"Spoon"
"Door"	"Tray"
"Eat"	"Glass"
"Cookie"	"Cup"
"Bed"	"Mama" (used for adults
"Potty"	and foster grandmother)
"Chair"	"Papa" (used for foster
"Socks"	grandfather)
"Shirt"	"Kool-aid"

Some of these words were target words on the traditional basic word list. Most of the words hold so much meaning for the children that it is easy to understand why and how they have become useful spoken words. The words used to teach "Listen" and later for "Do" or "Say" should be taken from this list. The objects and pictures used in training should also be selected from these lists.

The traditional basic word list can be used for more target words when a child is comfortably using the words most necessary in his daily life.

CHAPTER GUIDE

Attaching Meaning to Sound

    I. Hear-and-do.

   II. See-and-do. Add gestures and movement.

  III. Identifying activities.

     A. Find things around the child such as his bed, toy, potty, window.

     B. Use "Show me" activities.

     C. Play "Is Tommy here?"

  IV. Listening activities.

     A. Make noise and hide the noisemaker.

     B. Locate different noisemakers.

     C. Recognize the difference between noisemakers.

   V. Looking and listening activities.

     A. Select different toys on command.

     B. Touch the toy.

     C. Know the difference between two toys.

  VI. Use real objects.

 VII. Use miniature objects.

VIII. Increase the number of objects.

  IX. Use color photographs.

   X. Include action words such as "Put in," "Take out," etc.

  XI. Use music and rhythm for those who can tolerate it.

 XII. Make a list of each child's basic words.

     A. Words understood by gestures.

     B. Words understood without gestures.

     C. Words appropriately spoken by the child.

7

Developing Expressive Language

Receiving ideas of any kind or in any way is using receptive language. It would be impossible to know if a child receives any ideas from you without some sign from the child to let you know that the message was received. In TBA, the act of doing what you asked the child to do is a form of expression; his response in reply to your order is a form of expression.

Most of us think of "expression" as words spoken and used in the correct way, but there are other means of expression. When an infant learns to listen, he lets you know by wiggling all over if he likes something he hears, or by crying if he does not. He has learned to attach meaning to some sounds that reach him. His wiggles or cries are his expressions; he is telling you in his own way how he feels about what he heard.

Later when the baby holds up his arms to be picked up, he is telling you what he wants with a gesture. This idea starts inside of him; this is inner speech. It is his own idea and he tries to get his idea across to you.

When the idea and the way of getting that idea across start inside, from a child's storage of experience and without your asking, then he is truly expressing himself. Ideas can be expressed by moving (wiggling, making gestures, making signs, drawing, writing), by making sounds that have meaning (crying, screaming, moaning, grunting, humming, singing), and by using words. Expressing ideas of any kind or in any way is using expressive language.

Language must always have real meaning. A child should be taught to use spoken words rather than just mimic you. Down's Syndrome children can easily be trained to say words; sometimes it is difficult to move ahead from saying words parrot-style to using a word as a real tool for communication.

When a child succeeds in saying a word by mimicking you, he does get the feeling of saying the word and might remember how it was said. Be sure, however, that the word has meaning for him. A parrot doesn't really want a cracker when he says "Polly wants a cracker"; the parrot gets his reward from attention. If a child succeeds in saying quite a few words without meaning and has been rewarded too easily, it can become almost impossible to move him along from just saying words to *using* words. Using words to communicate is the goal.

Down's Syndrome children, in particular, can be shaped to say words and even to say color words (such as "Red" when shown a red chip or block). Such a child can be shaped to name and match quite a few colors, but unless he can find something red or yellow away from the block on the table in front of him, it is not useful word production. It is very hard to encourage the child to leave the success he is enjoying by being rewarded for just saying the right color name. It is better to leave color naming out until many other words are being used comfortably for labeling things and actions.

Words can occur spontaneously at any time during the TBA or receptive language training and it is important to take advantage of this by reinforcing any communication attempt, no matter how weak. Children sometimes approximate a word, such as "wa" for "water." If you suspect that the child's vocalization is an attempt to say a word, then reinforce it with an immediate reward.

TEACHING EXPRESSIVE LANGUAGE

When a child can identify things and let you know in some way that a word he is hearing or a gesture he is seeing has meaning to him, he is *expressing:* sending out an idea that has meaning and is usable to him. He may use gestures for a long time before he says words that name things or actions. Some children may keep on using gestures to get ideas across just like some deaf people use their hands to talk. Deaf people must receive all ideas through their eyes by lip-reading, reading printed words, or seeing "signs," a special way of moving hands or fingers to get ideas across. The exercises for capturing attention and creating eye-to-eye contact help the child use his eyes as well as his ears to collect ideas.

It may be necessary to settle for gestures and signing in some cases. Signing is the use of gestures to express ideas when spoken words can't be used. A pointed finger is signing, just as a pointed arrow is a sign that means "go this way." Some signs are learned quickly, such as "Yes," "No," "Eat," "Bed," "Go for a ride," "Go for a walk," "Wash hands." The language pathologist who works with you is the person to decide when to stop trying for spoken words and to start teaching some basic signing.

Labeling is attaching a word (or sign) to something or some action so someone else can get the idea. This is the do-and-say or see-and-say step in making spoken words useful in daily living.

Up to now, you have been teaching the child to listen and perform some action. Now you will try to get him to *say* the word for what he is doing. This is called do-and-say.

At first, you expected the child to respond with body action or by identifying objects or pictures by selecting, pointing, or touching. You have been teaching the child to listen and do.

During TBA, you used some words to describe action or movement. You did not expect the child to say the words after you;

55

you just repeated the action words each day for at least a month. Hopefully, the child imitates words at the end of this period. If he does, reward him immediately and say, "That's right, jump, jump."

If the child does not begin to imitate words after a month, you must begin to act out the pattern as you did with label words. Start with the word "Jump." Use the small trampolet or board and be sure you hold both the child's hands securely in yours. As the child jumps, say, "Jump, jump, jump" each time he jumps. As he steps or jumps off the trampolet say, "Down," rather emphatically. If the child shapes his lips to make a *J* sound or makes a *U* sound, reward him and say "Jump, that's right, jump." He is trying to say "Jump."

After a four-week period you should be getting good jumping action: the child jumps when you tell him to jump, making you feel quite sure he knows what the word means. If he is not starting to say "Jump" just to imitate you, then hold his hands as he jumps the first jump, stop him, smile, then say "Jump, say jump." Reward any efforts that could be the start of any sounds in the word "Jump," and keep trying.

Walk to soft, rhythmic music, hand in hand, saying "Walk, walk, walk, walk" in time with the music. Follow the same steps as you followed with the word "Jump." Introduce each new body action the same way, by naming the movement.

When the child can follow your command on how to move and can say the word for what he is doing, he has learned the first step in do-and-say. The words for direction, "In — out," "Up — down," "Over — under," etc., may be difficult but success in responding to these words with correct total body action will probably lead to attempts to say these words, particularly if the words have true meaning to the child.

Sometimes a child will say the right word by imitating. Reward him each time. He may start to use the word properly without imitation after his mouth gets the feeling and memory of saying the word for which he has been rewarded.

Your first goal is to have the child follow the spoken direction: to listen, to see-and-do. Your second goal is to have him follow the directions and say the word: to do- or see-and-say. This is *labeling,* the big step toward using words to communicate.

Some children do better if labeling is begun by using the big things they are already familiar with, such as real objects in the cottage: the bed, the window, the bath tub, the potty. Other children do better if labeling starts with small objects they can handle, like a toy bed, bath tub or potty for a doll house. Sometimes better attention and results come from using pictures of the real objects in the cottage. You must try each method with each child because no two are alike. You will soon learn which way works best.

Objects and people seen every day are best. For example, the water cooler may be very important, so "Water" might be good to start with. Words that have some practical value, such as "water," "bathroom," "bed," "bus," etc., should be used so that the child can use these words to get what he wants. Use words from the basic word lists.

Try to begin with an easy word that the child can see you say, such as "bed." Sounds made with the lips, such as *b, p, m, ch, j, w,* are easily seen. Do not try to have the child say a word unless you are sure he understands the word. This means he has done well during the receptive language training. Accept and reward any try that comes close to the word you are using, even lip movement. "B–" for "Bed" is a good start. Be patient, as you may say the word a hundred times before the child tries to say it and later use it.

Begin teaching the child only one word at a time. If you work with real objects in the cottage, take the child by the hand and go to his bed. Say "Say 'Bed'," touching the bed at the same time. Take his hand and help him touch the bed. Say, "Bed." Then smile at the child, touch the bed again, and say, "Say 'Bed'." If he even puts his lips together as if he were going to start to make a *b* sound, reward him and say, "Bed, that's right, bed." You may need to move his lips gently, helping him form a *b* sound, and repeating, "Bed, bed." Encourage him to watch your mouth as you say "Bed."

As the child learns to say "Bed," add a new word from the basic word list. Use a word for something you know he likes or something he likes to do. If you have no success with the first word, try another word from the list that you think he might like better. Do not work to teach him to say more than three or four words until you are sure he says these first words easily.

The child will likely say the word in imitation as you say it; that is, he will mimic the way you say it. This is natural, though it could be quite a long time, possibly several weeks, before he *says* the word all by himself. Keep on saying the word as you touch the object for a few days, then just touch the object and only move your lips to start to say the word. Reward him as soon as his lips move.

If you say, "What is this?" too soon, you will confuse the child. He hears you say, "What is this?" and you want him only to hear the sound of the name of the object. When he can say a few words appropriately, you can start using the question, "What is this?" or "Show me" when you want him to say "Bed."

Quite often a child will start to say and use a word you have not been working on. This spontaneous use is much to be desired. Quickly repeat his word, reward him, and use his word as often as possible.

Listen to the sounds a child makes during play periods. You may be able to hear some sounds he is using that have meaning to him. If you do hear a sound that you think might be almost a word to him, repeat it the way you heard it. If it does have meaning to him, his face will light up and he will seem to ask you how you learned that word! When a sound from the child gets his idea across, that sound has definite meaning to him; to him it is a word. You can help him say it better after you are sure he is using the sound meaningfully and comfortably. If you try too soon to help him say it better, he may give up and not try at all. Reward him every time he gets the idea across to you. Just knowing you understand his sound is a big reward to him.

If you work with pictures or toys instead of real objects, go about it the same way. Sit next to the child, or as close as possible, at a table or counter. Do not have anything on the table. Have the objects in a small basket on your lap and select two objects the child knows, such as a ball and a potty. Take the child's hand and place it on the ball. Say, "Ball, ball." Then put the potty on the table. Say, "Potty, potty," placing the child's hand on the potty. Then pick up the ball and say, "Ball, ball; Benny, *say* ball, ball." Be sure you reward the child if his lips move to form a *b*. Later, wait for a better response before giving the reward. Do the same thing with the potty.

Continue with the two objects for no more than three minutes. Then add another pair of objects and follow the same procedure.

When the child succeeds in saying a few words appropriately, he is rewarded by knowing his ideas are getting across. This reward helps him to want to use words and to keep trying. Usually when eight to ten words are being used comfortably and profitably, the child will start on his own to use words to express his likes and dislikes.

CHAPTER GUIDE

Developing Expressive Language

   I.   Review previous guides.
  II.   Reinforce best approximations of words.
 III.   List what the child expresses through gestures.
 IV.   Accept signing as expressive language.
  V.   Begin labeling activities and things
     A. Jump
     B. Do-and-say activities
     C. Do- or see-and-say activities
     D. Large real objects
     E. Small real objects
     F. Words starting with *b, p, m, ch, j,* and *w*
     G. One word at a time
     H. Say the right word in response to "What is this?"

8

Signing

USING MANUAL SIGNS

Many developmentally-retarded children do not learn to talk for any one of several reasons. Some may be deaf or hard of hearing. The deaf child usually has no speech because he could never hear sounds and so cannot imitate them. The hard of hearing child may hear a little but not enough to develop useful speech. Some children have brain damage or fears that keep them from talking.

Many of these children develop gestures that tell you about wants and needs, but you may be the only person who understands these gestures. One of the ways you can help nonverbal children is to teach them to use a simple sign language that you and all people working with the children will understand. Signing will open the way for these children to receive and express ideas.

Before you begin training in signing, you must choose a basic vocabulary. These words should include signs for colors, toilet, water, eat, drink, clothing, foods, hurt, and signs for all the activities in which the child is engaged. Whenever you use a sign, say the word at the same time. This is total communication. The word will probably not be repeated, but sometimes it is, and that is a big gain. Some basic beginning signs are shown on page 115.

Correct Use and Proper Placement of Hands

Since many persons will be involved in the signing program, it is necessary that each one use signs correctly. In order to be understood when using signs, there are several things that must be done properly.

When using signs, it is best to keep the hands as close to the body as possible and in the proper position. An example of improper placement can occur with the sign "see." Each of the two fingers is placed directly below the eyes, but if these fingers are placed anywhere lower than the nose, it is no longer "see," but "smoke."

Many signs are similar in movement and hand shape, and these signs must be kept as different and distinctive as possible. Any variation from the proper motion will only cause confusion, misunderstanding, and frustration. "Chair" could easily be confused with "name" if the fingers are not held properly. Confusion also will result if the fingers are spread apart; that sign is for "salt." Many problems can be avoided if each sign is very carefully made.

Signing too far away or too close can also cause difficulty in understanding signs. Visual handicaps, which will be discussed later, must be taken into consideration. Even if visual problems do not exist, errors in understanding the signs can result from improper body placement. Since the front of the body is used as the base for all signs, it is important to face the person being spoken to. The best communication is achieved when both persons engaged in a conversation face each other.

It is very hard to read someone's signing if it is jumpy and jerky. It is hard for the eyes to follow and just as hard to understand. As rhythm and smoothness are obtained, speed will come naturally. Forcing speed will only cause more problems.

Stressing the Manual Sign

When you begin using your hands to talk, you soon realize that even though you know what you're saying, it is not always understood as quickly by the child you're talking to. By exaggerating your signs, you will be more likely to get your message across and make the child feel less confused.

Make the sign large enough to be seen and understood. Small detailed signs are often not seen or are confused with other signs. "Come" and "go" are good examples of how to make a sign large. For "come" the arms should be stretched all the way out before you and brought all the way back to the body. "Go" should start with the extended forefingers next to the body, moving them away until the arms are stretched all the way out. Many children have visual problems, and making the signs large makes them easier to understand. Since it is difficult to make some signs large, stress these signs by repeating them several times. Simply bringing the clenched fists together is the sign for "shoe," but tapping the fists together several times helps in stressing the sign and making it clearer. "Money," "school" and "work" are other signs that can be repeated in order to make them understood. Signs should be made at a slow pace. Taking more time gives the child a better chance to understand the meaning of the sign. Exaggerating the time lapse between words also helps in separating the signs and avoids confusing several movements for one word.

Use body movements and facial expression, and say the word when you make a sign. Normally deaf people watch the face and not the hands whenever they are talking in sign language. Although it is doubtful that these children will eventually watch the face more than the hands, facial expression and body movements always help a child to understand. Signing such words as "good," "hurt," and "bad" will have much more meaning if you smile, squinch, or frown. When you use facial expression, you add much feeling that could not be expressed just using your hands. Tilting the head for "bed," closing the eyes for "sleep," and hunching the shoulders for "perhaps" will add much to your signing.

STANDARDIZING SIGNS

It is necessary to standardize the sign language you are using by using the same sign for the same word every time. Through a training program, signing can be taught to the entire staff. Learning to sign is worthless to the child unless he has trained receivers around him. This must include his own family as well as his teachers and classmates. Even the bus driver should be taught to use some basic signs.

Use the same sign for the same word. If different signs are used for a word, even if they are considered correct by different localities, it will only cause confusion. It will be difficult at times to teach just one sign for a word, but using more than one sign will cause twice the problem. If you always say the word you are signing, much confusion is avoided.

Use the signs that are most needed. The sign language vocabulary should cover a large portion of the activities that would occur in the child's environment. A general list of about 300 words will be sufficient to meet most needs. Of course, some children will learn more than 300 signs and, for some, other words will be necessary in order to meet specific needs. Then again, some children may need only a few words such as "come," "go," "sit down," "eat," "bed," "potty," "drink."

These signs will be basic in building a suitable vocabulary to be used with nonverbal children. Teach them what they seem able to learn.

Reinforce correct signs although the child may have developed his own gestures for certain words. Many children use gestures and pantomime to communicate their wants. Many of these gestures are different from the standardized language of manual signs. Although these gestures are different, it is not always necessary to deliberately change an incorrect gesture. Through consistent use of a correct sign and saying the word you are signing and reinforcing correct signs with praise whenever they are used by the child, the incorrect gesture will fade from use.

USING SIGNS AS A MEANS OF REWARD

Rewards, either praise or food, are used successfully in regular teaching, and rewards would work equally well with nonverbal children. There are ways to use manual signs to convey praise. Use the signs for "good" and "thank you." The sign for "mistake" can be used when errors are made.

Through the continuous use of signs as rewards, the child will discover that these signs have meaning as he learns how and when they are used. Using the sign for "good" will tell the child "you have done it right," and he will know that wonderful feeling of success. Again, if the sign has meaning, he will know more of what is expected of him. Seeing the sign for "mistake" should cause him to look again and find the correct answer.

Once a child begins to use sign language to express his pleasure and displeasure, it is important that these gestures be rewarded if appropriately used. This is the most crucial part of teaching developmentally retarded nonverbal children sign language. Once they begin using these signs without prompting and with meaning, you must be aware of what they are gesturing and you must respond correctly. By responding to the child's efforts to communicate by using signs, you are giving him the satisfaction of understanding, and this response soon becomes his reward.

In shaping the behavior of retarded children, verbal praise plays an important role, right along with the reward of small pieces of candy, cereal, and bits of fruit. With deaf children who cannot hear the sounds of praise, it is important that the signs of praise be used along with edible rewards, pats, and hugs. By pairing signs with things to eat and caresses, the child will understand the meaning of the signs, and signs can soon take the place of edibles. The nonverbal hearing child needs the same reward system.

TRAINING TECHNIQUES

Many deaf, hard of hearing, and other nonverbal children have been involved in training programs, with remarkable results.

Besides hearing difficulties, other problems, both physical and behavioral, can cause added burdens. Controlling behavior, consistency in sign training, manual-oral stimulation, and the use of visual stimuli are all part of training the nonverbal child.

Behavior Control

Behavior shaping has changed the lives of many children by helping them learn self-help skills such as dressing, eating, and bathing. By encouraging only the good habits and discouraging the bad, many behavior problems have been eliminated. In order to gain these results, the child's correct responses are rewarded with bits of food. The type of food used depends on the child's own likes and dislikes. At first any attempt, no matter how poor, was rewarded and approximations were judged. The smallest movement toward a desired response was always rewarded. Gradually, better attempts were demanded before giving a reward. As each correct response was made, the reward was given quickly. When sign language is taught, the same techniques are used, but every food reward is accompanied by the sign for "good." Also, nod the head "yes," and give a pat on the back. A smile is good, too. In order to train a child, it is important to gain and keep attention, discourage bizarre behavior, and reinforce desirable behavior.

If the child cannot hear, different means of gaining his attention must be used. If you are close, a mere touch or pat is sufficient. Waving the hands is good also. As deaf persons can feel vibrations, you can get attention by stomping your feet. If the child does not or will not look at you, it may be necessary to reward him every time he does give you his attention. Once you have gained this attention, formal sign training can begin.

The most effective means of discouraging unusual behavior is to ignore it. By giving attention to unwanted behavior, you encourage the child to repeat it. Withdrawing the materials you are using during the training session will also discourage bizarre actions.

Whenever a correct response is made, reward the child with candy, a pat or hug, and the "good" sign. Once the child realizes that when he gives the right response he gets a piece of candy, or something good, he will be more likely to respond correctly the next time. It is also important to use rewards outside the training period whenever the child shows good behavior. These rewards will encourage the child to use the correct behavior more often.

Training Periods

In order for the sign language program to be most effective, it is necessary to assign a certain time in which specific training is done. A quiet room or area should be used, with no distractions. The materials to be used for that session should be within easy reach.

Daily training sessions are very important. You need to spend at least 20 minutes in each training period, varying by several minutes from child to child depending on how quickly each tires.

You should keep a notebook to jot down new words covered each day, the child's behavior, and other important changes that occur during training sessions. This will help in planning future objectives and goals for each child. It will show what progress has been made and will help other aides working with the same child.

Manual-Oral Stimulation

It may seem strange to talk to someone who cannot hear what you are saying. Remember, however, that these children can *see* what is said. Also, some of the children involved in a sign training program will be able to hear quite well.

Speak clearly and loudly while signing. Many children will watch your lips and follow along with them. By speaking loudly and clearly and pronouncing each word with force, the youngster will be able to understand more of what you say to him. Many children are able to hear a little, and this verbal support will help them greatly. Speaking plainly to nonverbal hearing children will speed their learning.

Say the word as you sign it. The rate of signing and the rate of speaking should be the same. Saying the word and then signing it, or signing the word and then saying it, could slow the child's learning.

By using signs and words together, an association is formed between a certain group of sounds and a certain movement of the hands. This can also help many children by stimulating them to attempt speech. Children who rely on lip reading will be helped also.

Keep your mouth and hands always within eye range. Normally, deaf people usually do not watch the hands, but the mouth. For this reason, the body is positioned where both hands and mouth are readily seen by the child. These deaf children do not always focus on the mouth, but by keeping the hands and mouth in eye range, the movements of the jaw, lips, and tongue will help make a conversation understandable. For children who do not read lips, this technique will help them learn how sounds are made.

As the children begin to learn their signs, you should help them use the signs in their daily living activities so that they will have a useful comfortable means of communicating wherever they are.

Remember to reward every attempt (or try) as well as every success.

Use of Visual and Tactile Stimuli

The entire program for teaching sign language depends upon the child's ability to see. The child must also be able to control the movement of his hands, but he learns to make the signs by seeing the proper movements made and imitating what he sees.

In most training sessions, you will use real objects, miniature objects, and pictures of objects, along with the sign for the object and the word that is its name. The objects and pictures help stimulate the child to make the proper sign.

It is best to start with real objects that the child sees around him every day. These could include his own bed, the drinking fountain, a window, car, bus, tree, swing, a favorite toy, or flowers. Show the child the object, let him touch it, and then you say its name and make the proper sign at the same time. A child will learn more quickly if the sense of touch is employed as much as possible in teaching him signs.

Let the child see the real leaves being blown from a tree as you shake your finger, making the sign for tree. Let him sniff a flower; actually touch and turn a steering wheel in a car or bus. Not every sign can be learned this way, but the signs that can be learned by adding together the senses of seeing and touching and smelling will be learned more quickly, and give the child a good feeling of success. This combination of stimuli will help him to learn the process for making signs.

Using miniature objects such as doll house furniture, farm animals, plastic fruits and vegetables, and doll clothes is fun for the child and gives access to many objects which are otherwise unusable. Be sure these miniatures look as much as possible like the "real thing," and that they are familiar to the child and within his own experience.

If pictures are used, illustrate only one idea at a time. Stand them in a rack or against the wall to avoid glare. It is difficult for a handicapped child to focus his eyes downward. Use large pictures that are close in size to the object or scene they illustrate. Avoid pictures with too much detail, since they confuse the central object or idea you are trying to teach.

Communication Boards

If the child cannot control the movement of his hands well enough to make signs, an alternate technique — communication boards (also known as language boards) — are designed for individual children who do not talk and cannot use their hands as required in signing. This system uses a display board showing pictures, colors and, later, words that are needed to exchange ideas.

The most simple board would show, for example, only a glass of milk in one framed area and a cookie in another area. After the child has been trained to identify each picture (see Chapter 6), he learns to point to or touch the correct picture to show what he wants. You would say, "What do you want? Show me." At first, guide his hand to the right picture. Some children may need wrist or arm management to hold a hand steady enough to point. The boards become more and more helpful as the child learns to pick out from the display what he wants to tell you.

Communication boards may range from the ultra-simple, enabling only communication of basic needs, to electronic boards. The content of a board may include pictures, words, sentences, Blissymbols, numbers, alphabet, colors, etc. The layout of each board will vary according to the individual child. The language clinician should plan the make-up of the boards for each child and tell you how to go about using them. It's an exciting breakthrough for many children who could not tell you much of anything before learning to use a communication board.

CHAPTER GUIDE

Signing

I.   Gain attention.
II.   Have child match colors, objects, etc., whenever possible.
III.   Give sign for color, object, etc.
IV.   Ask for item using sign.
V.   Help child make signs.
VI.   Point to the item and have child sign object.
VII.   Show item, have child sign it.
VIII. Ask for item using signs.
IX.   Have child ask for the item using signs.

9

Evaluation of Communication

HEARING

It is necessary to discover if the child has enough hearing to develop receptive and expressive language. Deafness or a nerve related hearing problem would greatly limit both receptive and expressive language. Usable hearing is determined by asking the opinion of staff who work closely with the child and by informal testing. Most severely retarded children in a communication shaping program cannot be tested by a conventional hearing testing machine. The recent development of the Madsen Impedance Bridge, which directly measures middle ear functioning, tensor reflex, and other reflexes, has provided techniques to measure and evaluate the profoundly retarded without a response requirement. Experience has shown that those who work closely with the children can make a fairly good judgment of a child's hearing. In the Appendix is a sample form for the staff to use in estimating usable hearing for the development of speech (pages 92-93).

An easy test of hearing is to whisper the child's name while you are standing where he can't see you. Check both ears by whispering from both sides. Hold your hand near your mouth so the child does not feel the air move as you whisper. If he can hear his name whispered from three feet away, he probably has enough hearing to learn to speak.

Sometimes children do not respond to their name or to other spoken words, although they can hear. It is possible to determine this by using toy noisemakers. Noisemakers such as a small metal cricket, a small metal chime, and small bells can be used to estimate hearing. Set the child at a table in a quiet room with toys to attract his attention. Have one aide close by the table to observe the child's responses and another aide standing behind the child and out of his line of vision with the noisemakers. Sound the noisemakers behind and to one side. The child may indicate that he hears by turning his head towards the sound, or by just stopping his play for a second or two. A small eye movement towards the sound may also show that the child hears. Use the noisemakers on both sides to check both ears. The noisemakers may also be used to see if the child can locate sound by moving the noisemakers to different positions around the table.

If aides working with the child feel he can hear and he responds to noisemakers or whispered speech, he probably has enough hearing to learn to talk. If the cottage aides question whether the child can hear, and if responses are not always the same, then the child's hearing should be tested by a specialist.

FORMAL EVALUATION

When working with severely and profoundly handicapped children, evaluations and progress notes are necessary to determine where one is and what is the best direction to proceed. First, a speech and language evaluation should be conducted by a qualified language pathologist. (The speech and language evaluation form on page 94 of the Appendix has been used with severely and profoundly retarded individuals at Pinecrest State School.)

Charting

A program book should be made up for each child. The program book should include a form to record the date of each satisfactory attempt of an activity (see sample on page 95).

Using a form similar to the Total Body Activity Form (pages 96-97), an aide can chart progress from the beginning. By keeping a simplified chart up-to-date, any trainer will know exactly how far a student has progressed. Charting should not require an excessive amount of time to complete. Using these forms, a student's progress can be charted over time and his areas of success and difficulty identified.

The Language Developmental Scale (page 88) is very helpful in showing the child's progress, as well as in informing the trainer where the child is in comparison to a normal child in development of language skills.

The Four Week Evaluation Chart (page 98) is used to quickly show tongue movements, blowing and sucking activities, and response to commands. It provides an easy way to chart specific progress in identifying words, listening activities, and naming (labeling).

Lesson Plans

Daily lesson plans should be made up for each child, listing the activity, the reward to be used, and the time schedule. A sample form is in the Appendix, page 102. When an aide works with a child regularly, lesson plans are no longer always necessary. Lesson plans might then be made up only when an aide will be absent so a replacement can carry on the program.

For overall language evaluation, the Pinecrest State School adaptation of the North Jersey Training School Language Rating Form may be used (see Appendix, page 103).

Nursery Test

The direct care aide should complete a Nursery Test once every six months or once a year for a child to measure how well training is progressing. Local forms can be developed for each school or institution. Using this instrument, a progress report can be written. A sample Nursery Test Score Sheet is given on page 114.

LANGUAGE PROGRAM — PROGRESS REPORT

Under the guidance of Julia Molloy and Byrn Witt, Consultants, an intensive communication shaping program was designed. A manual was prepared in mimeographed form, and the techniques suggested by the consultants were attempted. In order to evaluate the communication shaping program, the North Jersey Language Scale was studied, tried and modified. The resulting instrument was called the Pinecrest Language Nursery Scale. The scale was used for residents in cottages who were to receive communication shaping training as well as residents of other cottages where we hoped the activities would be made possible.

Twenty-nine (29) residents were pre- and post-tested on the Pinecrest Language Nursery Scale approximately one year apart. All residents participated in some type of language training or communication shaping training. In order to administer the Pinecrest Language Nursery Scale, direct care aides had to be taught. An additional 209 children were pre-tested after the aides were trained. They were post-tested approximately a year after their initial test. Of the 29 residents who had already been pre- and post-tested, 12 improved in most categories. Table 1 shows the number of residents who improved in each category. About 50 percent remained the same in most categories. In the case of the motor response identification of miniatures, improvement was noticeable, but in encoding gestures, losses were noted.

It is difficult to explain why the residents become poorer in encoding gestures. The language program will be continued and perhaps when a larger number are post-tested, it will be explained.

Normative data are listed in Table 2 on 153 subjects by mental age. It is hoped that as the training program in communication shaping is continued, we will find an increase in percentage of items passed at an earlier mental age.

One hundred twenty-seven (127) residents benefited from language shaping directly. Three hundred sixty-five (365) residents experienced language activities indirectly as a result of the stimulation and concern throughout the Institution.

TABLE I

LANGUAGE NURSERY TEST RESULTS

N = 29

	IMPROVED	POORER	SAME
I. BODY IMAGE			
A. Echo	12	6	11
B. Naming	8	8	13
C. Identification	7	7	15
II. AUDITORY VOCAL PRESENTATION — **MOTOR RESPONSE IDENTIFICATION**			
A. Large Real Objects (LRO)	7	8	14
B. Small Real Objects (SRO)	6	6	16
C. Miniatures (M)	16	9	4
D. Colored Photos (CP)	9	8	12
AUDITORY VISUAL PRESENTATION — VOCAL RESPONSE			
Naming:			
A. L.R.O.	10	3	16
B. S.R.O.	10	6	13
C. M.	11	6	12
D. C.P.	12	5	12
Echo:			
A. L.R.O.	11	5	13
B. S.R.O.	10	6	13
C. M.	12	6	11
D. C.P.	13	4	12
III. VISUAL DECODING	10	9	10
IV. MOTOR ENCODING	9	6	14
V. COMPREHENSION OF COMMANDS	9	6	14
VI. ENCODING GESTURE	4	22	3

TABLE 2

LANGUAGE NURSERY SCALE

Mean percent number of items passed by Mental Age Level after 6 months of program.

MA	N	CA	IQ	ECHO	NAMING	IDENTI-FICATION	LRO	SRO	M	CP
						AUDITORY VOCAL PRESENTATION — MOTOR RESPONSE IDENTIFICATION				
.6-0.9	26	10.3	8.6	0	0	10	0	0	0	9
1.0-1.4	36	9.3	11.5	14	0	15	11	38	26	17
1.5-1.9	29	13.5	15.7	37	20	64	68	84	72	59
2.0-2.4	14	12.0	21.3	43	31	80	91	94	79	69
2.5-2.9	13	16.3	22.5	38	34	59	60	78	73	61
3.0-3.4	14	17.9	22.2	75	58	83	99	100	96	92
3.5-3.9	15	15.0	30.5	56	43	70	93	92	92	87
4.0	6	15.4	40.8	31	82	83	98	100	100	70
	153									

AUDITORY VISUAL PRESENTATION — Vocal Response

Naming				Echo			
LRO	SRO	M	CP	LRO	SRO	M	CP
0	0	0	7	10	0	0	1
0	0	0	0	0	0	0	0
17	22	16	15	28	26	21	18
35	38	24	26	39	31	29	36
29	36	36	30	35	81	39	37
55	59	56	46	55	59	58	49
43	49	38	54	51	56	50	62
50	57	59	52	53	61	59	58

VISUAL DECODING	MOTOR ENCODING	COMPREHENSION OF COMMANDS	ENCODING GESTURE
0	28	15	0
37	44	51	33
65	59	85	24
57	41	86	81
63	66	68	38
88	95	99	98
85	90	91	100
97	90	97	86

Plateauing and Regression

From time to time, children arrive at one level of development in their training and are unable to advance higher. Plateauing results from numerous factors. One factor is that the child is not ready for further advancement in terms of growth, maturation, or motor development. Children plateau because they have not reached the readiness level for the next higher skill. Plateauing also occurs when the trainer unknowingly takes a giant step or skips a small interim step to the next higher skill, or when the skill that the trainer is trying to teach requires an untaught or unrecognized interim skill. Lastly, a child plateaus because the trainer could not decide on the next appropriate step, so he switched to another skill sequence.

At times, you will find that a child is no longer capable of a previously-learned behavior. This is called regression. This always occurs when training is discontinued or interrupted for short periods of time. To learn a new skill, the child should be rewarded every time he performs the desired skill. To maintain a learned skill, the child should be rewarded concretely only at intervals, but always rewarded with a smile.

CONCLUSION

Teaching meaningful communication to a severely or profoundly handicapped child is a difficult, time-consuming process, but is one of the most important activities you can undertake. The rewards to both you and the child are immense, and well worth the time and effort it requires. Be confident that you will succeed, and you will — because you can *and because you want to.*

REFERENCES

Barrett, A. M. *When thinking begins.* Springfield, IL: Charles C. Thomas, 1973.

Bensberg, G. J. *Teaching the mentally retarded: A handbook for ward personnel.* Atlanta: Southern Regional Educational Board, 1965.

Dayan, M. Toilet training retarded children in a state residential institution. *Mental Retardation,* 1964, *2,* 116-117.

Ellis, N. R. Toilet training the severely defective patient: An S-R reinforcement analysis. *American Journal of Mental Deficiency,* 1963, *68,* 98-103.

Gardner, J. M., & Watson, L. S. *Behavior modification of the mentally retarded, an annotated bibliography.* Columbus, OH: Columbus State School, 1969.

Kephart, N. *The slow learner in the classroom.* Englewood Cliffs, NJ: Merrill, 1960.

Larsen, L. A., & Bricker, W. A. *A manual for parents and teachers of severely and moderately retarded children.* Nashville, TN: IMRID, Peabody College, 1968.

Molloy, J., & Matkin, A. *Your developmentally retarded child can communicate.* New York: John Day Book: Thomas Y. Crowall Co., 1975.

Teaching the mentally retarded — A positive approach. Atlanta, GA: National Medical Audio Visual Center (23 min., 16 mm black & white film).

Thompson, T., & Grabowski, J. *Behavior modification of the mentally retarded.* New York: Oxford University Press, 1972.

Watson, L. S. Application of operant conditioning techniques to institutionalized severely and profoundly retarded children. *Mental Retardation Abstracts,* 1967, *1,* 1-18.

Watson, L. S. *Behavior modification employee training manual.* Columbus, OH: Columbus State School, 1969.

Glossary

ACCELERATE. To increase or go faster. Also, to suddenly speed up, increase, or improve.

APPROXIMATION. To come as close as possible to doing something, such as a child trying his best to "skip" and almost doing it, or shaping his mouth to say a word and almost saying it.

ARTICULATION. The way sounds are put together to make words.

ASSOCIATION. Two or more ideas, things, or people doing something together.

ATTENTION. Fastening eyes onto something or someone, listening to some sounds, noticing some movement, some taste, smell or the feel of something.

ATTENTION GETTING. Finding ways to get someone to look, listen, or touch.

ATTENTION SPAN. The length of time a child can keep look-ing, listening, or doing something.

AUDIOVISUAL AID. A machine or tool that gives a picture and/or sound that helps get and hold attention and helps learning.

AUDITORY. Received in the brain through the ears: hearing, listening.

AUDITORY TRAINING. Helping a child learn to listen and to understand what he hears.

AWARENESS. Knowing something is going on, or someone or something is near.

BABBLE. Making sounds in a string or chain without saying words. Babble sounds usually start with a *b, p* or *m.*

BALANCE. To control the position of the body so it doesn't tip over and fall down.

BASELINE. The starting point. A measurement of what a child can do at the starting point of a training program.

BEHAVIOR. Anything a living thing does which includes move-ment, thinking, and learning.

BODY IMAGE. The picture a person has in his brain about his own body.

BOMBARDING. Attacking with many things in one or more ways, such as hearing, seeing, and touching.

BRIDGING SIGNAL. Something that will act as a "bridge" between completion of the act and the reward or reinforce-ment. It tells the child that a reward is forthcoming.

CARRIER PHRASE. Words put together leading to the main idea that is being worked on.

CARRY-OVER. Using something learned, away from the direct learning situation.

CHAINING. Teaching an entire behavior by conditioning and reinforcing each step separately and then bringing the steps together. Chaining also means putting words together to make phrases or sentences.

COMMANDS. Words or gestures that tell you to do something in a way that makes you feel you really ought to do it.

COMMUNICATION. Any exchange of ideas.

CONCEPTION. Putting together ideas to get a good answer. Knowing that the meanings of words can be used in different ways.

CONSISTENT. Always the same.

CONSONANT. A letter or combination of letters of the alphabet except the vowels a, e, i, o, u and sometimes y.

CONTINGENCY. What must be done to get a promised reward. A contract.

COORDINATION. Body parts functioning properly together.

CUE. That which reminds or brings attention to something.

DECELERATE. To slow down or stop a behavior.

DECODING. Getting the meaning from any sensation the senses bring into the brain.

DELAYED SPEECH. A child should say his first usable words about his first birthday and should put words together about his second birthday. If he does not follow this schedule, it is cause for worry.

DEPRIVATION. Not being allowed to have certain needed things, experiences or people.

DEVELOPMENT. The way people and things grow.

DEXTERITY. The ability to use the right hand, left hand, or both.

DISCRIMINATION. Deciding what you want to use because of the size, shape, color, action, or feeling of something; or deciding where you want to be, or what you want, or who you want to be with as it affects only you.

DISTRACT. To take attention away from what should be done or what should be paid attention to.

DROOL. Allow saliva to run out of the mouth.

ECHOIC RESPONSE. Repeating something just like it was heard, like an echo.

ENCODING. Putting ideas into appropriate action, gestures, or words.

ENVIRONMENT. Everything around you.

EXAMPLE. A pattern to follow or to copy.

EXPERIENCE. A happening; an activity that a person is aware of and remembers.

81

EXPRESSIVE.   Putting out an idea, a thought, a feeling.

EXTINCTION.   Eliminating a behavior by not reinforcing that which caused the behavior to occur.

FADING OUT.   The act of slowly changing cues to one's environment is called *fading*. If cues are removed, it is *fading out*.

FREQUENCY.   How often something happens or takes place.

FRUSTRATION.   The feeling of "I just can't do it."

GESTURAL LANGUAGE.   Exchanging ideas by using gestures or movement instead of spoken words.

GESTURE.   A movement (usually with hands) that sends an idea to another person without using spoken words.

GOALS.   Achievements to attain.

HEARING LOSS.   Imperfect hearing but not total deafness.

HINT.   An idea to help attain a goal.

IDEAS.   Thoughts, notions, and opinions existing in the brain.

IDENTIFYING.   Knowing and being sure that something or some person is just that thing or person and nothing else.

IMITATE.   Do something just like someone else does it.

INITIAL.   The first part; the beginning.

INNER LANGUAGE.   Thinking in the brain without saying any words or making any sounds.

INNER SPEECH.   Unspoken words that have meaning to a person.

INTERMEDIATE.   In between an easy and a more difficult task.

JARGON.   Sounds strung together that have some meaning to a child.

JOURNAL.   A written record of activities.

KINESTHETIC.   Starting, sustaining, and stopping movement.

LABELING.   Attaching a name to something or someone.

LANGUAGE.   A system to exchange ideas.

LATERALITY.   A side of the body that seems stronger or is used more comfortably or efficiently than the other side. Differentiating between one's left side and one's right side. Awareness of left and right within one's own body.

LEARN.   To profit from experience and remember so the experience can be used.

LEVEL.   A step, a platform, a plateau.

LISTEN.   Using the ears to hear by paying attention to the sound you are being expected to hear.

MEANINGFUL.   Significant; with its own meaning.

MENTAL AGE.   The age level at which the brain functions.

MOTIVATION.   A force or desire that makes a person want to do something.

MOTOR CONTROL.   Being able to control body movement.

MOTOR GROWTH.   The way one grows in control of the movements of the body.

MOTOR PLANNING.   Thinking about how to move the body appropriately.

MOVEMENT.   The result of a motor action that puts a body part into another place.

NAME.   The sound symbol that belongs to just one thing.

NAMING.   Attaching the correct sound symbol to just one thing. (Also called *labeling*.)

NEGATIVISTIC.   Refusing to go along with any suggestion, command, or idea.

OBJECTIVES.   Desired skills or ideas.

OBJECTIVITY.   Looking at the target behavior for its own value.

ORAL.   Anything to do with the mouth or with the sounds that come out of the mouth.

PALATE.   The roof of the mouth: the part between the teeth is the *hard palate;* the part that slants down over the tongue is the *soft palate.* If a child is born with the palate open down the middle, it is called a *cleft palate.*

PATTERN.   A plan or set way of doing something.

PERCEPTIVE.   Able to attach meaning to something.

PLAN.   A series of ideas put in order so a goal can be reached.

POSITIVE REINFORCEMENT.   Rewarding proper behavior or actions.

POSTTEST.   Testing done after the first test was given, to measure gain or loss.

POSTURE.   The way the body is held.

POTENTIAL.   The real ability that can be used.

PREFERENCE.   What a person would rather use or rather do.

PRESCRIPTIVE TEACHING.   Teaching planned to help problem areas of learning.

PRETEST.   A test done at the start of some planned teaching or activity to help establish a baseline.

PROMPT.   Assisting to get a correct response.

PROCEDURE.   The step-by-step way to do something.

QUALIFY.   To add words for special meaning.

RANDOM.   Wild motions or wild guessing without planning behind the action.

RECEPTION.   Receiving or taking in through the senses.

RELIABILITY.   Being able to depend upon something to occur again the same way.

REPETITION.   Doing something over again and again.

REWARD.   That which is satisfying and for which a person is willing to expend effort.

RHYTHM.   Repeated beat.

ROUTINE.   A planned sequence of events or experiences that is set and does not change very often.

SATIATION.   Having enough of anything to destroy interest or desire.

SATISFY.   Reaching an end result that fits the task.

SATURATION.   The limit of absorption; as much as can be learned at one time.

SCALE.   A measuring device.

SCHEDULE.   A plan for using time, or for things to happen according to a plan.

SENSORY.   Having to do with the way ideas and messages enter the body.

SEQUENCE.   The order in which things should be done.

SHAPING.   Molding simple behavior into a more complicated behavior.

SOCIAL.   Attributes or activities involved in getting along with people.

SOUND SYMBOL.   A sound that means something.

SPEECH.   Words that are spoken.

SPONTANEOUS.   Happening without help; ideas or actions starting inside a person.

STABILITY. The ability to be strong and level-headed.

STIMULATE. To make something happen.

STIMULUS. That which steers a person to a particular behavior.

STIMULUS CONTROL. When cues or stimuli control behavior.

SUBJECTIVITY. Allowing personal feelings to enter into judging an object, person, or activity.

SUCCESSIVE APPROXIMATION. A slow change in the contingency for a particular activity so that it becomes more like the final desired behavior.

SYMBOL. Something that stands for something else.

TACTILE. The sense of touch.

TASTE. The flavor of something that comes in contact with the tongue.

TOTAL BODY ACTIVITY (TBA). A planned program to teach a child to manage and control his body and which serves as a base for learning communication.

TECHNIQUE. A particular way of doing something.

TIME OUT FROM POSITIVE REINFORCEMENT. Not giving a reward when undesirable behavior occurs. This is usually done by restricting all possible stimuli which might be rewarding for a short period of time. Not punishment.

TOKEN. A symbol that stands for something else; i.e., money.

TONGUE THRUST. Pushing the tongue out when swallowing.

VERBALIZATION. Putting ideas into words.

VISUAL. The sense of sight.

VISUAL SYMBOL. A symbol whose meaning is seen rather than heard or touched.

VOCABULARY. A collection of all the words a person uses.

VOCAL. Sounds uttered, spoken, or sung so they can be heard.

VOCALIZATION. Making sounds with the voice.

VOLUME. How much anything holds, or the loudness or softness of a sound.

VOWEL. *A, e, i, o, u,* and sometimes *y.*

WORD MEANINGS. The ideas gotten from words that are heard or seen.

Appendix

DEVELOPMENTAL SCALE FOR LANGUAGE LEVELS

The developmental scale is intended to provide the teacher with standardized information regarding receptive and expressive language development in the normal child. It should not be used as a strict rule for the child with retarded development; the teacher must not compare language development between normal and retarded children with equal mental age.

RECEPTIVE LANGUAGE	APPROXIMATE AGE	EXPRESSIVE LANGUAGE
(Hearing and listening)		(Saying, doing, and signing)
Heeds bell	1 month	
	2 months	Differential cries for pain, hunger, discomfort
	3 months	Coos, chuckles, laughs out loud. Gives vocal expression to feelings of pleasure.
Notices sounds, especially those of human voice	5 months	Vocalizes in self-initiated sound play.
Turns to sound of bell without seeing it	6 months	Vocalizes several well-defined syllables. Crows, laughs, makes sounds for pleasure. Imitates sounds, babbles.
	7 months	Puts two sounds together, like "mama," "bye-bye."
Responds to "bye-bye" by waving "bye-bye."	8 months	Vocalizes eagerness and excitement.
	9 months	Vocalizes two syllables. (Second is repetition of first.)
	10 months	Makes sounds during play.
Adjusts to commands: knows what "Come here," "No," "Don't touch" means.	11 months	Says one word to name or describe something like "mama," "water," "bye."
Responds to "No," "Don't touch."	12 months	Two word speaking vocabulary.

RECEPTIVE LANGUAGE	APPROXIMATE AGE	EXPRESSIVE LANGUAGE
	15 months	Uses jargon and gestures. (Jargon is child's own made-up language. Likes talking to toys.
Points to nose, eyes, hair.	18 months	One-word responses include naming, exclamations, greetings. Half of vocabulary is names. Uses initial vowels, consonants (says first sound of words).
Can name and point to a part of body.	2 years	One-third of vocabulary.
Obeys simple commands: "Give me," "Put spoon in cup."		Sentence length two or three words; asks to go to toilet by verbal or gesture indication.
Can repeat four words from memory.		Uses "I, you, me" fairly well.
Can fill in words or phrases of poems or songs.		Refers to self by name, can tell what just happened.
Can tell what you cook on, what you sit on, what is good to eat.	2½ years	Names objects.
		Three-word simple sentences.
Child will "put one block on paper" upon command.		Vocabulary consists of ¼ nouns, ¼ verbs and pronouns.
Repeats two numbers.		Uses past tenses of verbs, plural nouns.
Can point to more objects by name.		Uses "I" in reference to self.
Can name something in pictures.		
Can tell what burns, what barks, what blows.		
Can give the objects of six actions such as what flies, sleeps, bites, scratches, swims.		
Repeats three numbers.	3 years	Uses three to four word sentences.
Responds to prepositions, "put the ball on the chair," "put the box under the table."		Can tell what happened in more detail.

RECEPTIVE LANGUAGE	APPROXIMATE AGE	EXPRESSIVE LANGUAGE
Can give the use of common objects, i.e., "What do we do with the spoon?" ("Eat.")		Adjectives, adverbs, pronouns, conjunctions increasing in use.
		When looking at picture books, will answer when asked, "What is he doing?"
		Articulation: Consonants mastered: *b, p, m.*
		Knows songs and rhymes.
Obeys simple commands, "Put the book on the table."	3½ years	
Names more things — pictures		Sentence length four to five words.
Can name more things when asked, "What do you use to ---" (like "lock the door.")		Better use of pronouns.
Can give good answer.		Articulation: Consonants mastered: *w, h.*
Can tell what is happening in picture.	4 years	Sentence length four to five words.
		Pronouns, prepositions, conjunctions, are used well.
Memory for sentences: "We are going to buy some candy for mother."		Articulation: Consonants mastered: *d, t, g, k.*
		Compound and complex sentences begin to appear.
Responds appropriately with gestures and words to "What do you do when you are thirsty, sleepy, hungry?"		Future and past tense in common use.
Carries out request with six prepositions (in, out, beside, behind, under, in front of).		Counts three objects.
Repeats four numbers.	4½ years	Parts of speech: 19% nouns, 25% verbs, 15% adjectives, 21% pronouns, 7% adverbs, and 13% other parts of speech.
Can follow three commands in order; carries out complex orders in three parts.		Consonant production 90% or more correct.

| | **APPROXIMATE** | |
| **RECEPTIVE LANGUAGE** | **AGE** | **EXPRESSIVE LANGUAGE** |

RECEPTIVE LANGUAGE	APPROXIMATE AGE	EXPRESSIVE LANGUAGE
		Consonant sounds mastered: *n, ing.*
Knows some things that are opposite: like "brother is a boy, sister is a girl."		Sentence length four to five words.
Can give a good answer to "What is a ball?"	5 years	Picks out and names red, yellow, blue, green.
Memory for sentences: can repeat a sentence of about seven words.		Sentence length four to five words.
		Can tell about things and action in picture.
		Can tell a story correctly.
		Can name penny, nickel, dime.
		Articulation: masters consonants *f* and *v*.
Vocabulary: can tell what several words mean.	6 years	Tells more about picture: responds to picture.
Knows the difference between a.m. and p.m. and answers question "When does afternoon begin?"		Average sentence length six to seven words.
		Says numbers up to thirties.
	6½ years	Articulation: voiced *l, th.*
Repeats five numbers.	7 years	Girls' speech is quite grown up.
Similarities: "In what way are _____ and _____ alike?		
	7½ years	Mastered consonant sounds *r, sh, ch,* and consonant blends such as *bl, dr, tr.*
Vocabulary (Binet L. Score)	8 years	Boys' speech is quite grown up.
Can tell what is silly about something.		
Can tell why some things are different and some things are alike.		
Remembers points of a story; can tell why some things happen such as "What makes a sailboat move?"		

STAFF OPINION ON LANGUAGE FUNCTION

NAME: _____

RECEPTIVE LANGUAGE
Do you think child hears? _____

How do you get his attention? _____

_____

Does child follow commands? _____

_____

(List commands he follows)

    1. _____

    2. _____

    3. _____

What does child do when a sudden unexpected sound is presented? _____

_____

Does child pay attention to routine sounds such as doors, toilet flush, shower,

food cart, food wrappers or containers? _____

_____

Does child ever cover his ears with his hands? _____

Does child mind you better if you use gestures as well as words? _____

_____

What gestures seem to work the best?

    1. _____

    2. _____

    3. _____

RECEPTIVE LANGUAGE *(Cont'd.)*

Does the expression on your face seem to help the child mind? _____

_____

What words do you use that you feel the child understands?

1. _____

2. _____

3. _____

4. _____

5. _____

EXPRESSIVE LANGUAGE

List only words the child *says*. Also *sounds* he makes that you understand. ____

_____

List words the child *uses* to get what he wants or needs. _____

Does the child succeed in imitating any sounds or words, either spoken or sung?

_____

What does he like best? _____

Food

1. _____

2. _____

3. _____

Toys

1. _____

2. _____

3. _____

Activity (Walks, rides, etc.)

1. _____

2. _____

3. _____

People

1. _____

2. _____

3. _____

SPEECH AND LANGUAGE EVALUATION

Name: _____ Sex: _____ Examiner: _____

Birthdate: _____ Date of Evaluation _____ C.A. _____

Intelligence Test (verbal) _____ Date of Test _____

    C.A. _____ M.A. _____

Intelligence Test (Performance) _____

    Date of Test _____ C.A. _____ M.A. _____

Other Tests: _____

Summary of Evaluation:

Hearing:

Speech Mechanism (see below)

Language
    receptive _____

    inner _____

    expressive _____

Speech Mechanism
    Articulators
    Lips: Impressions _____ Drooling _____

            Pucker _____ Swing right _____ Left _____

            Drink through straw: Yes _____ No _____

    Teeth:

            Contribution to speech disorder: Significant _____

                Nonsignificant _____

            Condition of teeth _____

    Tongue: Impression _____

            Control of tongue tip on vegetative level _____

            Extend _____ Retract _____ Elevate _____

            Lateralize _____ Left _____ Right _____

            Mobility _____

            Control of tongue on voluntary level _____

            Extend _____ Retract _____ Elevate _____

            Lateralize _____ Left _____ Right _____

ACTIVITY SHEET

LISTENING ACTIVITIES

Environmental Sounds

Speech Sounds

Lip and Tongue Exercises

Movement alone:

Communication Attempts (Speech)

TOTAL BODY ACTIVITY

NAME _____

COTTAGE _____

	Date, Examiner	Date, Examiner	Date, Examiner	Date, Examiner	Date, Examiner	Date, Examiner	Date, Examiner
Step in and out of box							
Step over barrier							
Crawl under barrier							
Crawl in and out of tunnel							
Step in and out of hoop							
Respond to commands							
Respond to rhythms							
Respond to music							
Throw bean bag							
Catch bean bag							
Ball handling:							
Roll							
Return							
Throw							
Catch							
Retrieve							
Bounce							

	Date, Examiner	Date, Examiner	Date, Examiner	Date, Examiner	Date, Examiner	Date, Examiner	Date, Examiner	Date, Examiner
Mat Move arms — out - in								
legs — out - in								
Lift legs								
Lift head								
Roll over								
Crawl								
Walk								
Run								
Go up and down stairs								
Walk line								
Walk beam								
Step over ladder rungs								
Step over obstacles (boards placed on course)								
Jump on trampolet								

FOUR-WEEK EVALUATION CHART

MONTH _____ YEAR _____

NAME: _____

RATED BY: _____

I. TONGUE MOVEMENTS (Mark as follows: 0 — Does not try; 1 — Tries but fails; 2 — Tries and succeeds occasionally; 3 — Moves slowly but accurately; 4 — Has no difficulty.)

Date											Comments
1. Out											
2. In											
3. Up											
4. Down											
5. Left											
6. Right											

II. BLOWING AND SUCKING (Mark as in tongue movements)

Date											Comments
1. Whistle											
2. Balloon											
3. Straw											

III. COMMANDS (Mark: N — Never; S — Seldom; A — Always)

Date											Comments
1. Sit Down											
2. Stand Up											
3. Come to me											
4. Clap your hands											
5. Step up											
6. Step down											
7. Don't touch											

IV: IDENTIFICATION (BODY)   Mark as follows: N — Never;   S — Seldom;   A — Always

Date	Identification	Echoic Naming	Naming	Comments
1. Hand				
2. Foot				
3. Mouth				
4. Tongue				
5. Lips				
6. Eyes				
7. Nose				
8. Ears				
9. Hair				
10. Tummy				

V: IDENTIFICATION (OBJECT)*   Mark as follows: N — Never;   S — Seldom;   A — Always

Date	Identification	Echoic Naming	Naming	Comments
1.				
2.				
3.				
4.				
5.				
6.				
7.				
8.				
9.				
10.				

*Objects of environment used in training are listed here.

FOUR WEEK EVALUATION CHART

NAME: _____   RATED BY: _____

Mark as follows: N — Never; S — Seldom; A — Always

Date				Comments
1. Comprehend simple questions.				
2. Combine words spontaneously.				
3. Use phrases.				
4. Use simple sentences. (predominantly nouns & verbs).				
5. Use verbs, pronouns, past and present.				
6. Use pronoun, "I" — sometimes interchanges "me".				
7. Answer simple questions.				
8. Ask questions. Ask "why".				
9. Use past tense and conjunction "and."				
10. Use grammatical sentences.				
11. Understand prepositions.				

Date				Comments
12. Use prepositions such as "in front of," "behind," and "back of."				
13. Use articles "a" and "the."				
14. Speak without infantile articulation.				
15. Sentences are compound and complex.				

Date				Comments
1. Sentence length in words — 1.2				
2. Sentence length in words — 3.1				
3. Sentence length in words — 3.4				
4. Sentence length in words — 4.4				
5. Sentence length in words — 4.6 (intelligible)				
6. Sentence length in words — 5.1				

LESSON PLAN

Lesson Plans for ———————————— Cottage ————————————

Date plan started: ———————————— Aide: ————————————

————————————

TOTAL BODY ACTIVITY

                               Reward Used   Time

SPEAKING MECHANISM

                               Reward used   Time

ATTACHING MEANING TO SOUND
(Auditory Training)

                               Reward used   Time

FAVORITE:
    FOOD   TOYS   PEOPLE   ACTIVITY

EXPRESSIVE LANGUAGE:

PINECREST STATE SCHOOL*
SPEECH THERAPY PROJECT

NURSERY TEST

NAME _____

DATES: 1)   TIME: 1)
2)   2)
3)   3)

ADMINISTERED BY: _____

RATED BY: _____

1. All ratings are to be: √   Right
                                 X   Wrong
                                 O   No Response
                                 ~   Random Vocalization

    Except for Naming and Echoic
    Naming, Ratings are to be: 1   Intelligible and correct
                                 2   Intelligible and incorrect
                                 3   Unintelligible vocalization
                                        (definite attempt at patterning)
                                 4   Random Vocalization
                                 5   No response

2. All actual words or incorrect responses of the child to any chance stimuli during the testing (but not part of the test itself) should be recorded on the margins of the test forms or the blank final sheet.

3. The test should be administered in the following order in two separate sessions. This may be varied, as necessary, at the discretion of the administrator and rater.

Session I

Section I   — Body Image
                Identification
                Echo
                Naming

*Adapted from North Jersey Training School Rating Form

Appendix

Section II   — Auditory Vocal Presentation — Motor Response Identification
                  Large Real Objects
                  Small Real Objects

                  Auditory Visual Presentation — Vocal Response Naming
                  Large Real Objects
                  Small Real Objects

Session II

Section II   — Auditory Vocal Presentation — Motor Response Identification
                  Miniatures
                  Colored Photos

                  Auditory Visual Presentation — Vocal Response Naming
                  Miniatures
                  Colored Photos

Section III — Visual Decoding

Section IV — Motor Encoding

Section V   — Comprehension of Commands

Section VI — Echoic Gesture

Section I

BODY IMAGE

    A. **Identification:** Examiner says: "Where is your mouth?" or "Show me your mouth," or "Point to your mouth." May try all three to elicit response.

    B. **Naming:** Examiner points to each body part. Asks child to name part. (Start Section B only after completing all of Section A.)

    C. **Echoic Naming:** Examiner names part. (Wait briefly for echoic naming).

Identification, Rate: $\sqrt{}$, X, O, or $\sim$ Naming, Rate: 1, 2, 3, 4, or 5

	A. Identification (on self)	B. Naming* (spontaneously)	C. Echoic Naming (check)
1. Hand			
2. Foot			
3. Mouth			
4. Tongue			
5. Lips			
6. Eyes			
7. Nose			
8. Ears			
9. Hair			
(Stomach) 10. Tummy			

*Phonetic Transcription — Optional

Appendix

Section II

AUDITORY-VISUAL PRESENTATION — MOTOR RESPONSE
Subsections A and B may be administered separately from C and D — at a different time and even a different day. (See instructions on front page for suggested order of administration.)

SUBSECTION A

Part I — Identification

1. Locate real objects in view of examiner and subject from a single point in room; ask the subject to show you item #1; "Show me the bed." Whether the child responds or not, ask for item #2. Return to single point.

2. Repeat procedure through item #10, being sure real object is in view. *If the child echoes or repeats the name of the item, score him for Part II.

Part II — Naming

1. Examiner touches one item at a time, and asks subject, "What is this?"

Part III — Echoic Naming

1. Examiner touches one item at a time and says the name of the object. (Wait briefly for echoic naming.)

SUBSECTIONS B, C, & D

Part I — Identification

1. Place item 1 and 2 before child, proceeding from child's left to right. Ask for item #1, "Give me the glass" . . . Whether the child responds or not, reverse visual order of items and ask for item #2. Remove items 1 and 2.

2. Repeat procedure — items 3 and 4.

3. Repeat procedure — items 5-6-7 (7-6-5) (6-5-7)

4. Repeat procedure — items 8-9 (9-8)

These procedures to be followed for B) Real Objects, C) Miniature Objects, and D) Colored Photographs.

Part II — Naming

1. Examiner picks up or touches one item at a time, places it before the child and asks, "What is this?"

Part III — Echoic Naming

1. Examiner picks up or touches one item at a time, places it before the child and names the object (wait briefly for echoic naming).

IDENTIFICATION, Rate: √, X, O, ~   NAMING, Rate: 1, 2, 3, 4, 5

	Part I	Part II	
a. Large Real Objects	Identification	Naming*	Echoic Naming
1. Bed			
2. Window			
3. Chair			
4. Pillow			
5. Water (Fountain)			
6. Blanket			
7. Potty			
8. Door			
9. Tub (Bath)			
10. Broom			

	Part I	Part II	
b. Small Real Objects	Identification	Naming*	Echoic Naming
1. Glass			
2. Spoon			
3. Shoe			
4. Socks			
5. Ball			
6. Pants Dress			
7. Shirt Shirt			
Boys Girls 8. Belt Panties			
9. Coat Brush			

*Phonetic Transcription — Optional

c. Miniature Objects	Identification	Naming*	Echoic Naming
1. Box			
2. Table			
3. Potty (toilet)			
4. Bed			
5. Chair			
6. Mirror			
7. Pig			
8. Horse			
9. Wagon			

*Phonetic Transcription — Optional

IDENTIFICATION, Rate: √, X, O, ∼   NAMING, Rate: 1, 2, 3, 4, 5

d. Colored Photos	Identification	Naming*	Echoic Naming
1. Glass			
2. Spoon			
3. Tray			
4. Ball			
5. Sock			
6. Toothbrush			
7. Chair			
8. Slide			
9. Window			
10. Door			
11. Water Fountain			
12. Fence			
13. Pillow			
14. Blanket			
15. Potty			
16. Broom			
17. Tub (Bath)			
18. Swing			
19. Tree			
20. Wagon			
21. Drum			
22. Bed			

*Phonetic Transcription — Optional

Section III

VISUAL DECODING (MATCHING)

Demonstration:

Present following objects in left to right sequence before child:

Real Objects

Rattle — Lollipop — Wrapped Candy

Hold up a second identical lollipop. Let child lick it once or twice, but then say *"Give me another one"* or *"Give me one like this"* and augment this with a gesture and facial expression indicating he look on table for another. Keep the first lollipop within the child's field of vision all the time, but if he wants another lick, encourage him to look at the items on the table. *Do not name the objects as you hold them up.* When the child seems to understand the nature of the task, proceed to the next items.

RATE: √, X, O, ~

	RESPONSE
1. **Real Objects** Small wooden block - cup - spoon Ask child "Give me another one" (Hold up a block)	
2. **Real Objects** Straw - wooden stick - small ball "Give me another one" (Hold up a stick)	
3. **Pictures** Drum - Dog - Boy "Give me another one" (Hold up the boy)	
4. **Felt Circles** Green - Yellow - Red "Give me another one" (Hold up red circle)	
5. **Plywood Cutouts** (all the same color) Square - Circle - Triangle "Give me another one" (Hold up the circle)	

Section IV

MOTOR ENCODING

"Show me what you do with this." (Present real objects — one at a time.) Present all.

Rate: ✓, X, O, ~

OBJECT	RESPONSE
1. Spoon	
2. Glass	
3. Shoe	
4. Bread or cookie	
5. Ball (solid color)	
6. Moveable toy (push or pull)	
7. Toothbrush	
8. Towel	

Section V

COMPREHENSION OF COMMANDS

Care should be taken that *no gestures or eye or other facial movements* supplement these vocal commands. The commands need not necessarily be given in the order listed, and should, as far as possible, be appropriate to the situation, without anticipating the child's own spontaneous intentions.

Rate: ✓, X, O, ~

COMMAND	RESPONSE
1. Stand up	
2. Throw the Ball	
3. Come to Me	
4. Put the Ball in the Box	
5. Clap Your Hands	
6. Go to the Mirror	
7. Go Potty	
8. Pick up the Cup	
9. Sit Down on the Chair	
10. Give me the Box	

Section VI

ECHOIC GESTURE

The examiner should sit alongside of the child during this subtest. The hand which the child uses to imitate the gesture would be noted, i.e., whether or not it is the same hand as used by the examiner.

Rate: $\checkmark$, X, O, ~

COMMAND	GESTURE
1. The examiner points toward the the light and says "Do this."	
2. The examiner doubles up fist and pounds desk twice saying "Do this."	
3. The examiner claps hands and says "Do this."	
4. The examiner shakes his head and says "Do this."	
5. The examiner rubs the top of head with palm of hand and says "Do this."	
6. The examiner slaps left knees with hands and says, "Do this."	

NURSERY TEST SCORE SHEET

Section I   BODY IMAGE

A. Identification

✓	X	O	~

B. Naming

C. Echo

1	2	3	4	5

Section II   AUDITORY VOCAL PRESENTATION —
MOTOR RESPONSE IDENTIFICATION

A. Identification
   a. Large Real Objects
   b. Small Real Objects
   c. Miniatures
   d. Colored Photos

✓	X	O	~

AUDITORY VISUAL PRESENTATION — VOCAL RESPONSE

B. Naming
   a. Large Real Objects
   b. Small Real Objects
   c. Miniatures
   d. Colored Photos

1	2	3	4	5

C. Echo
   a. Large Real Objects
   b. Small Real Objects
   c. Miniatures
   d. Colored Photos

Section III   VISUAL DECODING

Section IV   MOTOR ENCODING

Section V   COMPREHENSION OF COMMANDS

Section VI   ENCODING GESTURE

✓	X	O	~

SIGN CHART

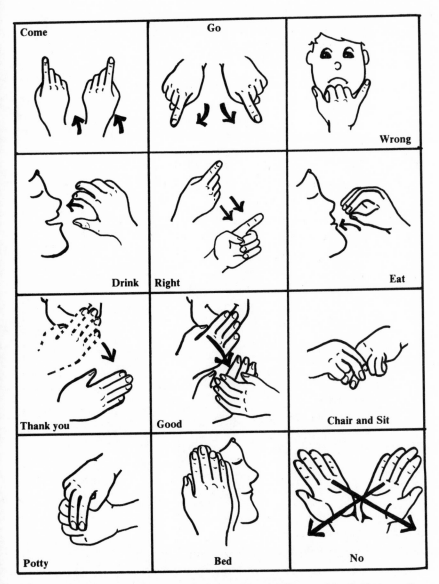

The above are basic beginning signs, as given in Owens, M., & Harper, B. *Sign Language,* a Teaching Manual for Cottage Parents of Non-verbal Retardates, Pinecrest State School. Pineville, LA 71360.